The Only Writing Series
You'll Ever Need

Grant Writing

A Complete Resource for
Proposal Writers

JUDY TREMORE & NANCY BURKE SMITH

adamsmedia
avon, massachusetts

Published by
Adams Media, a division of F+W Media, Inc.
57 Littlefield Street, Avon, MA 02322. U.S.A.
www.adamsmedia.com

Contains material adopted and abridged from
The Everything® Get Published Book, 2nd Edition
by Meg Schneider and Barbara Doyen,
Copyright © 2006 by F+W Media, Inc., ISBN 10: 1-59869-633-5
ISBN 13: 978-1-59869-633-2.

ISBN 10: 1-59869-869-9
ISBN 13: 978-1-59869-869-5
Printed in the United States of America.

J I H G F E D C B A

Library of Congress Cataloging-in-Publication Data
is available from the publisher.

This publication is designed to provide accurate and authoritative information with
regard to the subject matter covered. It is sold with the understanding that the publisher
is not engaged in rendering legal, accounting, or other professional advice. If legal
advice or other expert assistance is required, the services of a competent professional
person should be sought.

—From a *Declaration of Principles* jointly adopted by a Committee of the
American Bar Association and a Committee of Publishers and Associations

This book is available at quantity discounts for bulk purchases.
For information, please call 1-800-289-0963.

Contents

Introduction

The term grant writing is a misnomer. No one actually writes grants. Those who seek funding write proposals; those who give funding write grant agreements and checks. But despite this fact, grant writing is the term everyone uses to describe the process of writing a proposal for funding a nonprofit organization's programs, operations, or construction projects. And grant writer is the term that everyone from the nonprofit sector will understand when you use it to describe your work.

By itself, reading a book will not make you a competent grant writer. Applying what you learn will. Practice will. Asking questions will. And you must start somewhere. *The Only Writing Series You'll Ever Need: Grant Writing* provides a solid base of knowledge from which you can learn, practice, and develop intelligent questions to pose to seasoned professionals. This is a comprehensive how-to book that draws on the expertise of grant-writing professionals. You'll receive advice throughout the book from foundation program officers, grant reviewers, and a number of experienced grant writers. You'll read success stories, and you'll read stories about failures so you can learn to avoid the pitfalls. You'll get the know-how you need to effectively complete grant proposals to obtain the funding you need, to establish and build a thriving freelance grant writing business, or to qualify for a full-time, paid staff position as a grant writer in a large nonprofit organization.

This is your first step into this rewarding, satisfying career. Enjoy the journey, and good luck!

Chapter 1

Grant Writing 101

Grants are gifts made by a charitable-giving foundation or the government, most often to a nonprofit organization; that is, an organization designated a 501(c)(3) by the Internal Revenue Service (IRS). Grants are most often made to support the operations, special projects, or other activities of a nonprofit organization for a specific period of time. Grant proposals are submitted as requests for grant funding. Proposals include a narrative, forms, and attachments. It is the grant writer's responsibility to create, complete, and compile these documents.

What Is Grant Writing?

Grant writing has become the popular description of the process of writing proposals for funding, but it always comes down to this: No one actually writes grants. Those who seek funding write proposals applying for grants; those who provide funding write requests for proposals (RFP), grant agreements, and checks to projects that answer their RFPs and meet their standards. Hundreds of thousands of nonprofit organizations are looking for funding and thousands of grant providers are looking for projects to fund; but only a few hundred matchmakers bring them together, i.e., the grant writers.

What Does a Grant Writer Do?

Grant writing is the term everyone uses to describe the process of writing a proposal for funding a nonprofit organization's programs, operations, or construction projects, but a grant writer does far more than write proposals. A grant writer studies the philanthropic landscape of her community, enrolls to receive e-mail notices of grant funds, understands how to search for foundation and government grants, and knows how to cull through the search to select the most appropriate candidates. She is also a creative problem solver, a detail-oriented project supervisor, and a strong writer with a knack for brevity and clarity.

Who Applies for Grants?

While some individuals, such as inventors, and some businesses—particularly those in product development, research, defense, and construction—apply for grants, nonprofit organizations account for the majority of grant seekers for one simple reason: They need grants to develop new programs or sustain operations. In general, the following people involved with nonprofit organizations write grants:

- **Executive Directors:** In smaller nonprofit agencies, the work of grant seeking and grant writing is often assigned to the executive director.
- **Fund Development Officers:** Larger organizations often hire a fund development officer to seek and write grants.
- **Program Directors:** On occasion, you'll find program directors assigned responsibility for seeking grants to support the organization's programs or ideas, usually because the nonprofit's board of directors requests that staff pursue a specified number of grants or raise a specific amount of money through grant writing in any given year.
- **Freelance Grant Writers:** As executive directors of nonprofits have become busier and busier, the need for professional grant-writing services has grown consistently in the past several years, and shows no sign of slowing.

Is Grant Writing the Same as Fundraising?

No, each has distinct responsibilities. A grant writer is most often a writer with a specialty, though she may also do fundraising. A fundraiser may write grants as part of his job, but he is usually a person on staff who is assigned to general fundraising duties.

Fundraising duties can include nurturing long-term donors, developing candidates and plans for bequests, planning and executing fundraising events or speaker series, managing a database of donors, developing year-end and midyear letter campaigns, and other similar responsibilities. Larger organizations usually have someone on staff assigned to fundraising, and often that person is called a development director.

While many development directors can and have written grants, they become so busy with the other requirements of their jobs that grant writing becomes a sideline for them or something they seek from an outside source, such as a professional grant writer.

Common Cents
Foundations are prohibited from making grants to individuals. Instead, individuals with needs such as housing, transportation, counseling, or health care must seek those services from a nonprofit organization. The nonprofit organization, in turn, seeks funding from grantmakers to provide those services.

Who Provides Grant Writing Opportunities?
Some individuals and businesses write grants, but your primary market for freelance grant writing is the nonprofit sector. Among those applying for grants are the following groups:

- Religious organizations
- Social service agencies of all kinds
- Schools
- Hospitals and clinics
- Governmental units (some also solicit and fund grant proposals)
- Colleges and universities
- Police/fire departments

- Public-access media
- Arts and cultural organizations

What Does One Have to Do to Become a Successful Grant Writer?

Above all, to succeed as a grant writer, you must do four things both well and consistently.

1. *Feel empathy for your readers.* That means always writing directly to an audience. Learn who will be reading your grant proposals—often either a program officer at a foundation or a volunteer in a government office. Take care to understand what they need to know and how best to explain it to them.

2. *Always meet your deadlines.* If the grant arrives past the given deadline, even an hour late, it will not be reviewed! You may be able to resubmit the same grant to the same granting organization, but it's very likely that the next deadline will be a year or more away. Your nonprofit client will not be pleased; the organization may have been counting on that money for its next budget cycle.

3. *Thoroughly read and follow instructions.* This is more important than having a good writing style, good client relations, or even a successful grant-writing track record. While foundations are not as stringent, if you don't follow the instructions contained in the requests for proposals (RFP), many government offices will toss your unread proposal into the trash.

4. *Be a good "test taker."* You must be able to read questions thoroughly, analyze the question for clues to the best answer, and provide the answer that best responds to the core of the question. A common downfall of many grant writers is that they answer questions with information they want to tell the granting agency, rather than provide information the granting agency is requesting.

Interpreting the questions is the first step in writing a successful grant proposal and a skill that you'll perfect with experience. Focus on your audience and respond accordingly.

Insider Tip

Whether you are writing to guidelines or an RFP, the grant proposal is formulaic; it includes instructions that, in the case of RFPs particularly, must be followed exactly. You also must use the accepted language and approach set forth by your reading audience.

How Does One Look for Grant Opportunities?

Typically, one finds grants in one of two ways:

1. **Reactively:** As a response to a Request for Proposals (RFP).
2. **Proactively:** By searching for matches between foundation guidelines and your nonprofit organization's mission.

Government funding is most often accessed through an RFP process. Foundations sometimes issue RFPs for specific projects or initiatives, but most often present guidelines describing the location and types of organizations and projects they are interested in funding.

What Are the Different Types of Grants?

Grant proposals are most often written to seek funding for a specific project within a larger organization and are usually one of the following types:

- Capital: Funds for construction, acquisition, or renovation of buildings
- Programmatic: Funds to support staffing, equipment, and other items that are necessary to launch a special project
- Operational: Funds to support ongoing operations, such as utilities, ongoing staffing costs, etc.

Insider Tip

Some foundations are beginning to change their guidelines to look for ways to fund operations in nonprofits that are vital to the community or that have demonstrated "best practices" in their fields. However, most foundations still prefer to fund unique projects developed in response to a community need.

What Makes a Grant Proposal Successful?

There are two key factors that often determine whether or not a grant proposal is successful:

1. It provides a creative response to a problem or need.
2. It demonstrates potential for sustaining the project and its outcomes after the grant period ends.

A project and/or the organization proposing a project must have most of the following:

- Strong and recent data to support the need for the project or to describe the problem to be addressed
- An experienced project manager or other lead person such as the executive director of an organization
- A history of fiscal responsibility (or, if a new organization, comprehensive plans for fiscal oversight)
- A response (project description) that clearly addresses the identified need or a solution to the stated problem
- Collaboration with others in the community
- Community-member involvement in identifying the problem and the solution
- A plan for sustaining the project and/or the positive outcomes from the project after the grant period

Projects Must Fulfill a Genuine and Pressing Need

Projects that don't address a real and pressing community, state, or national issue are not fundable. They might be creative. They might have strong possibilities for collaboration with potential partners. They might appear to address the priorities of a funder. But they will fall short unless the need is documented with supporting data.

Projects Must Have Potential for Sustainability

A second major concern of funders is the ability of the nonprofit organization to support the program after their grant funding runs out. Though grants do not need to be repaid, the leader of a nonprofit organization must think like the small business owner and be creative in developing ways that a project can earn revenues sufficient to continue without grant funds. Planning for sustainability can be very complex and difficult, but documenting the potential is vital when seeking grant funds.

Chapter 2

Follow the Money

Our government predetermines the types of projects and programs that need public support and then, through its various federal agencies, identifies exactly where the funding should go. The grant-seeking process starts when those agencies issue RFPs to nonprofit and governmental agencies in each of the states.

Government Funding Sources

The federal government issues Requests for Proposals (RFPs) to determine which of the various local and state programs that meet its predetermined requirements should be funded. That money is allocated from the government to its federal departments, such as the Department of Housing and Urban Development or the Department of Education, to be used in each department's various grant programs.

Often, the funded programs are available year after year, but when there's a change in leadership, priorities shift and money is often allocated to new priority categories and departments. Many grant programs go on for years, so you will have more than one opportunity to submit a proposal for funding or to resubmit a failed proposal.

School districts receive announcements issued by their state and the federal Departments of Education; large mental-health agencies are notified by the Department of Health and Human Services; and police departments will be given notice of grants available from the Department of Justice. As you develop these larger nonprofits as long-term clients, they'll send you the RFPs and ask whether they are qualified to pursue the grant program or whether the proposed program is appropriate for their needs.

Search Government Sites

Another way to review federal grant RFPs is to search the government's grant website: *www.grants.gov*. You can use program titles, departments, key words, or Catalog of Federal Domestic Assistance (CFDA) numbers assigned to each RFP to find available grants.

You may also sign up with Grants.gov to receive regular notices of newly released RFPs. These notices offer a brief description of the grant program and a link to the request for proposals. If you are enrolled with Grants.gov, you will sometimes receive e-mail update notices when deadlines, funding levels, or instructions change between the date of the RFP release and the due date for applications.

Insider Tip

If you are working as a freelance grant writer, you can review RFPs on your own through Grants.gov, and call your clients and potential clients when you think one of the RFPs matches their requirements. While they are not obliged to ask you to write the proposal, they may well reward your notice with an assignment.

Visit Your Local Congressional Representative

You can also access an office copy of the National Register at your local congressional representative's office. It contains all proposed grant opportunities for the upcoming year, regardless of which federal department is issuing them and regardless of whether it's secured funding or the actual levels of funding listed.

The Register is published or updated annually, but is not distributed widely. Instead, a one- or two-page announcement is mailed to pre-established mailing lists approximately ninety to 120 days before the grant deadline. The summary announcement contains a brief description of the program, its *Federal Register* number (CFDA number), the requesting department, a list of legal entities that may apply, the URL of the full RFP, and either an application or a telephone number so you can request an application package.

Philanthropic or Organizational Funding Sources

Besides the government, philanthropic organizations, such as local foundations or the United Way, are a rich source of grants. Occasionally, in addition, people of wealth bestow grants without using a formal philanthropic organization or a grant-seeking process. A good grant writer is aware of these individuals in his or her community, but because the needs and interests of these individual philanthropists vary widely—as do the best ways to approach them—we will not focus on them in this book on grant writing.

Basically, however, you typically find three major types of foundations:

1. Large family foundations
2. Corporate foundations
3. Community foundations

If you want to pursue these avenues, it's important to identify the following:

- Their primary focus and specific philanthropic goals
- Their regional parameters
- Board members and their areas of responsibility
- How often—and when—they meet to make decisions about grants

Insider Tip

You can locate opportunities by meeting with board members, reviewing catalog listings of local philanthropists, researching foundation 990s (tax statements indicating charitable gifts and their amounts available at *www.guidestar.org*), and talking with other clients about their experiences in local grant seeking.

Some basic aspects of philanthropic, community, or corporate foundations that will help you understand the process are as follows:

- The major foundations have regular meetings in which they discuss projects and their planned portions of giving.
- Many of the smaller foundations wait to see what the corporate foundation does. They've come to understand and respect the staff person's approach to review and due diligence.
- When there's a really large capital project (such as an arena, convention center, or large university installation) that requires full community support, it becomes more difficult to get other special projects funded from the traditional sources.
- Staffs of foundations can't make promises or assurances on behalf of their boards.
- Changes in staffing (especially at the director levels) and trustee-board membership can affect decisions and/or delay decisions.
- The foundations publish their values and mission statements and expect you to address the ways that potential projects fit with their vision and values.

Foundation Requests for Proposals

Sometimes foundations issue RFPs, which are often available either on the foundation website or through the Foundation Center *(www .foundationcenter.org)*, which may allow you to sign up to receive regular notices of foundation grant announcements. The announcements contain information about eligibility, a deadline, a brief description of the program, and a link to additional information, as shown in the following sample announcement.

CALIFORNIA COMMUNITY FOUNDATION INVITES LOS ANGELES ARTISTS TO APPLY FOR COVER-ART AWARD

Deadline: May 4, 2007

The California Community Foundation's (CCF) (*www.calfund .org*) Cover-Art Award is designed to support an emerging Los Angeles artist working in painting, drawing, or printmaking by purchasing an artwork that best reflects the foundation's annual theme: "Arts and Culture in Diverse Communities." This year's theme embodies CCF's goal to support initiatives that expand access to the arts for low-income populations, recognize non-traditional art forms among various cultures, and leverage the arts as a means of revitalizing neighborhoods. The foundation will feature the winning artwork in its 2007 annual-report cover, invitations, and other publications, and a limited-edition lithograph.

Cover-art award guidelines and application instructions are available at the CCF website.

RFP Link: *http://fconline.foundationcenter.org/pnd/10006747/calfund*

Government RFPs

Foundation RFPs vary in their information, but government RFPs usually contain the following information:

- Purpose
- Issuing agency/department
- Criteria for the program
- Total grant funds available and range of prospective grant awards
- Eligibility criteria for applicants
- Statements that must be signed by the applicant (regarding the enabling legislation, nonsupplanting, public comment requirement, etc.)

- Deadline
- Mailing instructions
- Outline of proposal content
- Points available for each section of the narrative
- Rubric (a chart of judging criteria and scoring) or other selection criteria for judges
- An application kit containing budget forms, cover sheets, and assurances
- Appendices/documents such as State Single Points of Contact, resources, call for reviewers, etc.

Insider Tip

You may not deviate from the outline in the RFP—ever! If you don't follow the outline exactly, you can be assured that a grant proposal will be awarded funding, but it won't be yours. Remember, volunteers are often reading and scoring dozens of proposals at a time. They must be able to find the information where they expect to find it to assign it a proper score.

As a grant writer, you are most concerned with four sections:

1. The eligibility criteria. You want to check it first to ensure that your employer or client meets all criteria for applicants, or that, with partners, they can meet the criteria.
2. The deadline. You want to identify the deadline and develop your plan working backward from it.
3. The outline of content. This third section is the most critical part of the RFP; think of it as the writer's instructions. Pay close attention to these instructions, and don't deviate from them.
4. The review criteria. When you've completed your draft, you'll want to have it reviewed by peers and others both within and outside your organization. You do this to ensure that the narrative meets the highest level of the rubric scale.

Grant-Source Searches

Since RFPs, or at least announcements of their availability, are generally sent to qualified applicants, it's likely that your clients or employer will identify these grant sources for you or that you've found an appropriate grant opportunity through the Foundation Center or Grants.gov. But when it comes to compiling lists of other fund sources for your own files, you have a big job ahead of you.

To find foundation and other grant sources, you must check catalogs, software databases, and the Internet. As you begin to build your own knowledge base by asking for guidelines for various projects, you might consider putting foundation sources and their focus in a file cabinet (or electronic file) for easy reference or constructing a database that allows you frequent review.

Common Cents

If you intend to write grant proposals as a full-time pursuit either as a contract writer or as part of your job, it would be wise to organize information about fund sources in ways that make sense to you. Then, block out time on your calendar for annual or biannual updates to funder information. Foundations often review their program guidelines and change them without notice to potential grantees.

Regional Associations of Grantmakers

The Foundation Center lists many U.S. foundations and information about them. In addition, catalogs and CD databases of foundations are available through organizations called the Regional Associations of Grantmakers (RAGs). Different RAGs cover different regions of the United States. You'll have to pay a fee to get these resources from your RAG, but they are worth it when you consider the time it would take you to hunt down every source on the Internet, and when you want to zero in on funders that cover a specific geographic area.

RAGs publish catalogs that list only those foundations that are members of the organization. The listings contain the following information:

- Name and address of foundation (usually in alphabetical order)
- Contact person
- Donor
- Purpose of the foundation
- Limitations (what the foundation will not fund)
- Fiscal year (the time in which the foundation must pay out its 5 percent)
- Assets
- Typical annual expenditures (includes grants and foundation operations)
- Grants made in previous year by focus area
- Range of grant funding
- Deadlines for submission and/or decisions about grants (grant cycles)
- Means of approach (letter of inquiry, request guidelines, submit full proposal, etc.)
- Typical grant size
- Officers and trustees

Following is an example of an entry in a RAG catalog.

XYZ FUND
P.O. Box 1
Somewhere, USA   123-456-7890
Contacts: John Doe, Foundation Manager
Donor(s): John Smith

Purpose and Activities: Support for health-care agencies, humanities, human-service agencies, public benefit, and religious organizations.

Fiscal Year End: 12/31
Assets: $1,234,567
Expenditures: $75,975

	Total	Somewhere, USA
Grants	$65,000	$25,000
Number of Grants	50	18
Humanities	5.00%	4.26%
Education	2.50%	4.26%
Health Care	11.33%	16.17%
Human Services	32.83%	30.64%
Public Benefit	13.33%	
Religion	35.00%	44.68%

Grant Range: $1,500–$15,000
Typical Grant Size: $3,500

Application Procedure: Initial approach with letter describing purpose of grant and tax-exempt status verification.
Funding Cycle: Grants made in January of each year
Officers and Trustees: USA Bank
EIN: 123456789

The RAG catalogs (which may also be published and cross-referenced in an interactive CD) include such additional information as lists by geographical area of giving or lists by subject- or focus-area for giving.

You'll also find lists from the Council on Foundations, or on special CD/DVD research programs, such as those published for universities or medical-research facilities that may be of use.

Insider Tip

In some catalog entries, the foundation states that it "gives to preselected organizations only." They are not open to reviewing unsolicited requests, so do not submit your grant proposals to them unless someone makes direct contact with the donor and has his or her permission to submit.

How to Begin Your Search for Grant Opportunities

To narrow your search using a RAG catalog, refer first to their index of subjects or areas of interest. For instance, if your client or employer is a women's health service, refer to the index of grantmakers in medical research, mental health, or general health, and also to the index of foundations that focus on women's issues.

Next, refer to the individual foundations listed in those subject areas. Look at their limitations. If a foundation generally limits its giving to a specific city or region that your agency is not a part of, cross that foundation off your list of possible prospects. If the foundations are listed as giving to "preselected organizations only," find out if your organization has any connection through friends, staff, or previous funding. If not, cross these foundations off your list, too.

Now, look at the range of grant funds and the allocation to health or women's issues to get an idea of what each foundation might do to assist financially. Look up the best prospects, in terms of shared focus and size of awards, on the Internet or by using the contact information. Then write to request guidelines from each of your final prospects, or, if possible, download guidelines from the Internet.

Once you have all the information about appropriate foundations and the size of the grants they tend to give, develop a plan for approaching them. Be sure to note such things as means of approach. (For instance, will you stress that your organization fills a health-care gap in your community or that it addresses critical women's health issues?) Also, note deadlines for submission and decision-making, and the amount you can or should request.

Common Grant Application Format

The following sample guideline was developed by a Regional Association of Grantmakers (RAG) for use by any foundation within the geographical area of the RAG. Common grant applications generally have most of the same questions you will be asked to respond to in other foundation grant proposals; therefore, it's smart to do one of these first so you have some text for subsequent proposals to other funders.

COMMON GRANT-APPLICATION FORMAT

Please provide the following information in this order. Briefly explain why your agency is requesting this grant, what outcomes you hope to achieve, and how you will spend the funds if the grant is made.

A. NARRATIVE

1. Executive Summary

- Begin with a half-page executive summary. Briefly explain why your agency is requesting this grant, what outcomes you hope to achieve, and how you will spend the funds if the grant is made.

2. Purpose of Grant

- Statement of needs/problems to be addressed; description of target population and how they will benefit.
- Description of project goals, measurable objectives, action plans, and statements as to whether this is a new or ongoing part of the sponsoring organization.
- Timetable for implementation.
- Who are the other partners in the project, and what are their roles?
- Acknowledge similar existing projects or agencies, if any, and

explain how your agency or proposal differs, and what effort will be made to work cooperatively.

- Describe the active involvement of constituents in defining problems to be addressed, making policy, and planning the program.
- Describe the qualifications of key staff and volunteers that will ensure the success of the program. Are there specific training needs for this project?
- Long-term strategies for funding this project at end of grant period.

3. Evaluation

- Plans for evaluation, including how success will be defined and measured.
- How evaluation results will be used and/or disseminated and, if appropriate, how the project will be replicated.
- Describe the active involvement of constituents in evaluating the program.

4. Budget Narrative/Justification

- Grant budget; use the Grant-Budget Format that follows, if appropriate.
- On a separate sheet, show how each budget item relates to the project and how the budgeted amount was calculated.
- List amounts requested of other foundations, corporations, and other funding sources to which this proposal has been submitted.
- In the event that we are unable to meet your full request, please indicate priority items in the proposed grant budget.

5. Organization Information

- Brief summary of organization's history.
- Brief statement of organization's mission and goals.

- Description of current programs, activities, and accomplishments.
- Organizational chart, including board, staff, and volunteer involvement.

B. ATTACHMENTS
1. A copy of the current IRS determination letter indicating 501(c)(3) tax-exempt status
2. List of Board of Directors with affiliations
3. Finances
   - Organization's current annual operating budget, including expenses and revenue.
   - Most recent annual financial statement (independently audited, if available; if not available, attach Form 990).
4. Letters of support should verify project need and collaboration with other organizations. (optional)
5. Annual report, if available.

INFORMATION INCLUDED IN A COMMON GRANT APPLICATION

Date of Application:

Legal name of organization applying:

(Should be same as on IRS determination letter and as supplied on IRS Form 990.)

Year Founded:

Current Operating Budget: $

Executive Director:

Contact person/title/phone number (if different from executive director):

Phone Number:

Address (principal/administrative office):

continued

City/State/Zip:
Fax Number:
E-mail Address:
List any previous support from this funder in the last five years:

Project Name:
Purpose of Grant (one sentence):
Dates of the Project:
Amount Requested: $
Total Project Cost: $
Geographic Area Served:

Signature, Chairperson, Board of Directors
Typed Name and Title
Date

Signature, Executive Director
Typed Name and Title
Date

GRANT-BUDGET FORMAT

Below is a listing of standard budget items. Please provide the project budget in this format and in this order.

A. Organizational fiscal year:
B. Time period this budget covers:
C. For a CAPITAL request, substitute your format for listing expenses. These will likely include: architectural fees, land/building purchase, construction costs, and campaign expenses.
D. Expenses: include a description and the total amount for each of the budget categories, in this order:

	Amount requested from this organization	Total project expenses
Salaries		
Payroll Taxes		
Fringe Benefits		
Consultants and Professional Fees		
Insurance		
Travel		
Equipment		
Supplies		
Printing and Copying		
Telephone and Fax		
Postage and Delivery		
Rent		
Utilities		
Maintenance		
Evaluation		
Marketing		
Other (specify)		

E. Revenue: include a description and the total amount for each of the following budget categories, in this order; please indicate which sources of revenue are committed and which are pending.

	Committed	Pending
1. Grants/Contracts		
Contributions		
Local Government		
State Government		
Federal Government		
Foundations (itemize)		
Corporations (itemize)		

Individuals		
Other (specify)		
2. Earned Income		
Events		
Publications and Products		
3. Membership Income		
4. In-Kind Support		
5. Other (specify)		
6. TOTAL REVENUE	$	$

You're finally ready to begin preparing your submissions. You should take the most complex proposal outline first. In it, you'll create responses to sections that you can use again and again on the other proposals, such things as the need statement, program description, evaluation plan, and other sections that have to be tweaked only slightly to fit the focus or emphasis of the other foundations.

Common Cents

As with RFPs, when applying for foundation funds, you must follow the instructions for submission (the outline contained in the guidelines) to the letter. Most foundations have established procedures for reviewing proposals and providing careful consideration by the right person at the foundation. If you deviate from their procedures or instructions, you may harm your chances of getting the proposal to the right person.

Foundation Grant Guidelines

Larger foundations generally issue grant guidelines, which are available by request or by search. They contain critical information for framing your grant proposal, including the following:

- Background/brief history of foundation
- Categories for funding/focus areas, with brief descriptions of types of programs

- Means of approach (such as letter of inquiry, meeting with funders, arrangement for site visit, full proposal requested)
- General requirements for funding
- Instructions for submission (outline of required sections)

"Cold Calling" Versus Responding to RFPs

Remember, there are two basic approaches to seeking grants: responding to requests for proposals or "cold calling" on foundations. In the former instance, you receive a request for proposals that clearly outlines the types of projects the funder is seeking and the requirements for each project. Then you work with your employer or client either to develop a new program that responds to the requirements or to modify an existing program to meet the requirements in the RFP.

Most often, the programs described in the RFPs are those that have been found to work in other communities or that the funder wants to explore through several demonstration projects because they show great promise for systemic change. In these cases, you must design a program that is similar to or exactly like the one the RFP describes; the goals of your program and the goals of the funder must be the same.

A "cold call" is when you go to a foundation, either in person or in a letter of inquiry, describe the need you've identified in the community that is not being met by another agency, and tell what your organization would like to do about it.

Insider Tip

A cold call is the only way that you will seek funding from a foundation that does not issue RFPs—in other words, from most foundations. It is also an opportunity for you to educate local foundations about a new need in your community, and to position your client as a responsive, engaged participant in coalition building and program activities.

You'll find that area foundations are keenly interested in learning about new needs in their geographic areas, and in responsive, creative programs that can help meet those needs. Cold-call grants can be extremely successful, and you'll feel great that you helped launch a program that's sure to be positively evaluated.

Chapter 3

Government Grants

Government grants are tax dollars redistributed to programs in your community. As such, they can be made by any entity that collects taxes: federal, state, and even local city or county governments. In general, the larger the government, the larger the fund available for grants and the larger the individual awards for projects.

Local-Government Funds

Local governments are your city, township, county, regional coordinating body such as a water district, or other such mechanisms. Local governments rarely have grant opportunities, and those that do provide only limited programs. But they do issue RFPs.

RFPs That Aren't for Grant Programs

Local governments are more likely to issue requests for proposals that are actually for work they wish to have completed. For instance, the city council or similar unit of local government might decide they need to build a new parking lot. They will send the job out for bids and call the process a "request for proposals," but of course, this is not a grant program.

Local Grants with Pass-Through Money

Don't cross local government off your list of grantors, however, because sometimes they receive larger grants from the federal government that they can redistribute locally, such as Community Development Block Grants (CDBG) or Local Law Enforcement Block Grants (LLEBG). The local government determines the priority issues to address with these funds and then issues requests for proposals to address those issues.

Block-grant Funding

Block-grant funding comes from a source other than the local tax base. Usually it's state or federal money. Block-grant programs are often broad in scope and the issues they cover, such as housing, elder care, child welfare, and health. In addition, these programs are likely to be offered annually, and can be used as a source of operational funding for nonprofits that meet the criteria.

Insider Tip

Block-grant funding has become more scarce in recent years. And, even though a local government grants the money, grantees must comply with federal reporting requirements. Many now require extensive quarterly reporting on progress toward achieving outcomes.

State-Government Funds

Grants from the state are among the easiest to apply for and receive. You'll find that your state is close enough to communities to have an understanding of what's going on and the problems they are having, yet large enough to provide grants in sufficient amounts to address problems that have been identified.

You can find state grant opportunities in nearly the same way as you find federal-government grants: by going from department to department. Most states have a website that lists departments. Pages within each department contain information about upcoming RFPs.

Some grants are awarded on what appears to be an "it's-your-turn" basis rather than merit. For example, a state department of education might give funding to different school districts on a rotating basis. When that's the case, it's better not to apply for the funding every time it becomes available; you'd be better off waiting four or five cycles, then trying again.

Intermediary Funds

State or federal governments occasionally provide funds to a non-profit organization in your community, which the nonprofit then regrants to smaller nonprofit organizations. The intermediary is usually a larger, well established nonprofit such as Family Independence Agency, United Way, your community foundation, or your workforce development board.

When this happens, the local agency usually receives some of the grant as compensation for reviewing the mini-grant proposals, distributing the grant dollars, and ensuring that all reports and evaluations are submitted on time to the granting agent.

Intermediary funding is always granted for a specific purpose, and made to a local agency, because that agency knows more about needs in the community and the reputation of various service providers.

Community Development Block Grants (CDBGs), for example, are meant to be spent locally, and are used to develop projects that respond to specific community needs. Block-grant money is passed from the federal to state government. The state awards some grants to rural or smaller communities, and passes the rest of the money to larger city governments and lets them administer their own programs.

Federal-Government Grants

You will find that federal grants are where the money is and where the work is! Federal grants are meant to launch big programs; that's why awards can range from grants of less than $10,000 to grants of several million dollars.

Federal-government requests for proposals are published in the *Federal Register* (or Catalog of Federal Domestic Assistance), announced at various department sites on the Internet, and available at *www.grants.gov*. In addition, qualifying organizations often get advance notice of grants appropriate for their agency.

Some federal grant programs have been offered annually for decades, and are provided to designated agencies based on their progress reports and annual reapplications.

Insider Tips

All federal grant applications require a DUNS number, which is the nonprofit organization's Dun and Bradstreet (D&B) number. You can apply by telephone or Internet for a DUNS number. D&B provides financial information about your organization to the federal government, eliminating the need for you to attach lengthy audit reports.

New Grant Programs

Other grant programs are relatively new. Think about the new funding that became available once Congress passed the Homeland Security Act of 2002. This program increased funding already available to qualifying law-enforcement agencies through grants made by the Department of Justice. For the first time ever, firefighting units were also eligible to receive federal funding so that they could build up their capacity, purchase equipment, or receive additional training.

Insider Tip

When the federal government opens up a new grant program, such as the Homeland Security Act, it often means that fewer dollars are available for other grant programs. Often, particularly after an administration change, some grant programs are phased out and funding available for grants is redistributed to new programs.

Why You Should Watch Trends

Unless you are applying for designation and annual funding that is relatively stable, you should watch trends and allocations to the federal departments. When there is a large allocation made to one federal department, it's likely that large grant opportunities will be coming up within the year.

One-Time Opportunities

There are many one-time grant opportunities available from the federal government. These are usually multiyear awards—often of more than $1 million—given to demonstration projects throughout the nation.

Common Cents

The success of a new program funded by a large-grant award can be short-lived if you don't plan for the continued funding you'll need to keep the project going after the grant funds are spent. Planning for sustainability—for funding and outcomes—should be a part of every grant writer's expertise.

Federal Register

The Federal Register contains all requests for proposals, from all federal departments, that are issued in a given year. It must be voluminous, but most writers have never seen the entire Register. Instead, you will receive or download individual RFPs for individual grant programs.

If you receive an RFP package in the mail, it is usually bound and saddle stitched as a small booklet; online, it comes as a simple PDF file. It contains all the information found in the *Federal Register* about that particular grant program, including the following:

- Program number (CFDA number)
- Enabling legislation
- Purpose of the grant program
- Outline for your narrative
- Evaluation criteria judges will use to select the programs that are funded
- Forms and assurances (that the organization practices equal opportunity or has an environmental policy, for instance)

- Listing of State Single Points of Contact, when contact with them is required
- Instructions for forms
- Instructions for appendices
- Mailing instructions and addresses

Sometimes the booklet also includes frequently asked questions and responses and/or government contact information so you may ask questions by e-mail or telephone.

More often, you can download RFPs from the department's website. However, the package is not complete as a single downloadable file. You must download the RFP (usually listed by program title) and the forms (usually called "application package") separately. You also may choose whether or not you want to download additional pieces of information, such as frequently asked questions or other background information.

Over the past few years, the federal government has developed Grants.gov, which makes it easier now to get notices of funding and to search all departments through the search engine, but also requires grant-seeking organizations to preapply for access to the complete RFP package, a process that sometimes takes several weeks. Also, different departments are limiting applications for some programs to online submission only.

Insider Tip

Register your nonprofit organization with Grants.gov even if you don't think you'll be applying for a grant in the coming year. When you do find a grant opportunity, this will be one time-consuming hurdle out of the way.

Paper submissions for federal funding are becoming rare, and the online submission process requires you to open, close, complete, and submit a dozen or more different documents and can be confusing and time consuming. Be sure to plan at least a day for uploading, and, to be safe, try to plan this activity for the day before the deadline in case the system goes down.

Other Sources of Information

Most reputable nonprofits are on mailing lists to receive notification of upcoming grant opportunities. They are also often contacted directly by the local, state, or even federal department with which they work. But you can also search for government programs and RFPs on your own.

How to Go About It

A good search engine is the grant writer's best friend. Key words that will help you find government grants include the following:

- The purpose of your program or project (for example, lead hazards, school violence, prosthetics)
- The name of the department (be sure to specify "U.S." or name of state first to avoid getting a long list)
- The name of a similar program you know that has received funding. (When you search this way, you are likely to find out the name of the grant program they used and which department issued it.)

If your web-surfing skills are weaker than you'd like, start out with some of the websites set up especially for grant writers. In addition to listing private, corporate, public, and community foundations, they often include federal agencies that have issued RFPs. Usually, you can search these sites by categories or topics.

At the very least, you won't be wasting time filtering through a lengthy list of grant topics pulled up by a search engine, only to discover that half the sites contain only news releases while the other half list grants with deadlines that have already expired.

Insider Tip

Your local representative's office can help keep you informed about upcoming RFPs. Members of Congress often have a local office as well as a Washington, D.C., office, and your hometown staff is there to assist constituents. They will be willing to put you on a mailing list or a computer listserv so you can receive important announcements.

Bookmark Your Results

It can take a while to locate different departments and agencies that issue RFPs, so be sure to bookmark sites that you know you'll want to return to. Also bookmark sites from where you downloaded an RFP, so you can refer to it throughout the writing process. Why do you want to do this? Sometimes deadlines are extended or modifications are made to the RFP, and the only way you will have of finding this out is to watch the website for updates.

Chapter 4

Foundation Grants

A private charitable foundation engages in charitable giving from its "corpus," money endowed to the foundation by a wealthy person, family, or corporation.

Funding from a Foundation

Charitable private foundations are required by tax law to pay out, through grant making, 5 percent of the total corpus (endowment plus earnings) each year. They usually invest their endowment funds. In years that the stock market does well, they earn more than the 5-percent payout requirement and are able to build the corpus of the foundation. In years that their investments, overall, earn less than 5 percent, they must dip into the corpus to meet the payout requirements. Poor earnings in a single year won't affect a foundation's corpus or its ability to award grants, but if the market continues to decline in subsequent years, those foundations that have no means of income other than earnings from investments will suffer, and so will the nonprofits that they fund. While there are variations in type and size, in general, grant-making foundations are either private foundations or grant-making public charities.

Private foundations are nongovernmental, nonprofit, grant-making organizations managed by a board of trustees or directors that make grants for charitable purposes. They include corporate foundations, family foundations, private independent foundations, and operating foundations.

Grant-making public charities are 501(c)(3) nonprofit organizations that derive their funds from multiple donors, have a charitable purpose, and make grants. They include community foundations and public foundations.

Corporate Foundations

Although they are often linked with the founding corporation, corporate foundations are a separate legal organization subject to the same rules and regulations as other private foundations. Profit-making businesses, usually large corporations, establish corporate foundations to enable them to support projects in communities where they operate manufacturing plants, retail outlets, and other direct business. They are most interested in helping organizations in the communities where their employees live, though sometimes they expand grantmaking into communities where their customers live as well.

Corporate foundations have a board of trustees usually is comprised of current and retired corporate leaders. Staff often includes an executive director who reviews grants and makes recommendations to the board.

A corporate foundation is different from a corporate-giving program. The former has an endowment through which it earns income and makes grants. A corporate-giving program, on the other hand, makes grants of money or products based on its annual earnings. The gifts, therefore, fluctuate from year to year and may not be available at all during lean years.

Insider Tip

Direct-giving programs do not accept grant applications, and they are not part of the endowment entrusted to the corporate foundation. Gifts of money and goods are allocated from the annual profits of the corporation.

Family Foundations

The largest group of private foundations is family foundations, which are usually established by one or two donors. Family foundations ensure that future generations continue to practice philanthropy and are set up so that the endowment upholds values the donors believe are important. Most founders are successful entrepreneurs who want to use their fortunes to support the communities in which they and their families live. In return, they receive substantial tax benefits from the federal government.

Family foundations may be operated by a local bank, by the founder, by family members, or by a staff hired for that purpose. When a bank is in charge, grant proposals are mailed to a contact person at the bank. Staffed foundations will have an executive director and, as the corpus grows, will hire additional program staff. The board of trustees, which makes decisions about grantmaking, is usually composed of family members and sometimes includes third- and fourth-generation descendants of the donor. There also may be representatives from the community who were asked by trustees to serve on the board.

Some family foundations are established to make gifts to the same organizations the donor has supported for years. These types of foundations generally do not accept grant applications from non-profit organizations that have not been preselected for funding. Some family foundations serve in this capacity for only a couple of generations, then they become so large that they must broaden their grant-making focus or endow the preselected charities directly.

Private Independent Foundations

Family foundations are a subset of private foundations, and many private independent foundations have derived from the growth of a family foundation. The differentiation between a private independent and family foundation is the composition of its board, and, informally, the size of its corpus. In a family foundation, the majority of the trustees are family members; in a private independent foundation, trustees are those selected from the community for their expertise in or shared values with the foundation program areas. Private foundations (including family and private independent foundations), collectively, make nearly 90 percent of all grants made annually by foundations in the United States.

Common Cents

There are operating foundations, but they do not make grants. Instead, they exist for one purpose, such as finding a cure for a disease, and commit their endowments to that effort and their own operations (including building the corpus through investment).

Community Foundations

Community foundations are a great example of strength in numbers. They are established by a number of donors in a community, and continue to grow through new gifts to the corpus such as direct donations, legacy gifts, or annual donations. All community foundations are focused on a specific geographic area and do not make grants to organizations that are outside of their geographic focus.

Insider Tip

Do not apply for a grant from a community foundation that is in a different geographic region or city than that of your nonprofit client. Individuals set up these foundations to restrict their grants to organizations within their own communities.

There are more than 500 community foundations in the United States, all of which restrict their giving to the community in which they were founded or, at most, to the state in which they were founded. Their boards are comprised of community leaders who often include representatives of the major banks and law firms in the city. A new trend is to include some representatives from area nonprofit organizations. Community foundations work hard to keep their boards a diverse mix of individuals to reflect the composition of the overall city or region.

Foundations Within Foundations

One of the operational hallmarks separating a community foundation from family, private independent, and most corporate foundations is that a community foundation both raises funds and makes grants. They also hold, administer, and grant money through separate "donor-directed" foundations.

Insider Tip

You need to submit only one grant proposal to a community foundation to access funds held in a small foundation or trust. Part of the job of community-foundation staff is to match your needs with the interests of donors and make recommendations for funding. Sometimes you can get two grant awards with one proposal.

The grant-making process for these donor-directed funds is separate from the programs operated by the community foundation. Different boards and different values guide their giving. These smaller foundations within the community foundation benefit from having the community-foundation staff provide fiscal and grant-making oversight.

Public Foundations

Public foundations are generally small foundations established for a specific purpose, such as women's issues or church funds. They raise and grant funds as a grant-making public charity.

Other Sources of Grants and Funding

There are also other places to find grants, such as:

> *Discretionary Funding*: Family foundations and large independent foundations often have set amounts of discretionary funds—grants that can be awarded on the decision of one person, rather than an entire board—for program officers, presidents, and some board members. Read their annual reports or call the foundation

to learn who has control over discretionary funds and how you can request them. These small grants can be quite easy to get, as you only have to convince one person of the value of your proposed project.

United Way/Community Trust: United Ways are not endowed and, thus, are not considered foundations. Through annual fund drives, they raise funds that are then granted to programs and organizations selected, most often, by a group of community members.

Billionaire Foundations

There are between fifty and sixty private family or independent foundations that have assets of more than $1 billion and make millions of dollars in grants annually. They are staffed with numerous program officers and often have communications departments, presidents, vice presidents, financial officers, and other departments and staff similar to that of a large corporation. Their sophisticated operations and programming can make the private independent foundation more difficult to reach, especially if the geographic or social reach of your program or activity is narrow.

Many of these larger billionaire foundations are now focused on world issues, such as developing philanthropy and a nonprofit sector in emerging democracies, finding a cure for HIV/AIDS, or saving the rain forests in South America. Your nonprofit must have a really creative solution to a perplexing systemic problem and be as highly sophisticated in its operations as the billionaire foundation if you are to be successful in approaching these foundations.

Requesting Proposal Guidelines

A good way to identify foundations in your area is to request a catalog or CD from your Regional Association of Grantmakers (RAG). RAGs provide services to all the foundations within a region and develop catalogs that list them, often by city, alphabetically, and/or by type or program area.

Once you've identified the foundations that operate in your area, if you want to learn more about the foundation for future reference, request the guidelines by telephone or simply download them from the Internet. If, however, you have a particular project you intend to propose, you should write a letter. Briefly—preferably two paragraphs or less, no more than one page—describe the project you hope to submit, then close by requesting a copy of their guidelines. In this way, the foundation can help you assess whether they'll be interested in receiving a proposal. And—a big bonus—they sometimes even send a small donation without you ever having to submit a full proposal.

Proposal Guidelines

Proposal guidelines provide some or all of the following useful information:

- Name of a contact person and telephone number(s)
- Description of program areas (the types of projects the foundation is interested in hearing about)
- Restrictions, or those projects, geographic areas, or types of organizations the foundation does not fund
- Range of grant awards and average grant award
- Assets of the foundation
- Previous projects the foundation has funded
- An application form
- An outline for a proposal narrative
- A list of required attachments for the grant proposal
- Deadlines for submission
- General indication of the time it takes from submission to approval or denial

- Foundation history, mission, values, board roster, or anything else that will help you learn what motivates their giving

Other Sources of Information

While you are exploring the range of foundations in your area, you may also be interested in learning more about foundations in the United States. Besides the Foundation Center website, a great source of information to help you explore is the Council on Foundations (COF), a national organization that supports philanthropy in the United States and provides services and publications to member foundations.

You may also wish to use the Internet to download the guidelines of your targeted foundations, but do so only for information gathering. If you have a project in mind, you really should request guidelines or write a letter of inquiry to make sure you aren't wasting your time. If the foundation is not interested in receiving a full proposal, they will say so. That prevents you from wasting your energy on behalf of a project the foundation knows its board will not consider funding.

Chapter 5

The Right Source

You want to be able to search out funding sources for special projects and, often, for operating funds. In this chapter you'll learn more about sorting through the vast amount of information available and narrowing your field of prospects.

When Is a Government Grant Appropriate?

Governments cannot be solicited for funds; instead, you must rely on matching your project with an appropriate RFP. Watch for RFPs not only from the most obvious department—such as Department of Education grants for school districts—but also from other departments. You might find an opportunity from the Department of Justice, for instance, that will allow a school district to apply for funding to provide drug- or violence-prevention programs.

Also work with others in the community. Federal grant providers nearly always want to know as much as they can about the nonprofit infrastructure in your community. Who's doing what? Where is the potential for duplication? Where is the potential for partnership and cost savings? While many of the larger foundations are also interested in multiagency approaches to community problems, the most likely source for funding to allow such an undertaking is the federal government.

When Is a Foundation Grant Appropriate?

Foundation grants are most appropriate for local projects, especially those from organizations the foundations have worked with in the past or for projects in which the foundations have a high interest.

In one community, for example, nearly all the foundations support agencies that provide services for young children, including child-abuse/neglect prevention, early education, and children's health and nutrition. The community foundation also sponsored a task-force study on children's issues of children in the community. The study recommended a new interagency approach treating those who experienced child-abuse. Because of the community foundation's stature, several other funders joined in. Together they launched a new program that, in its ten years of existence, has enjoyed relatively stable funding from all of the original funders and others in the community.

Foundations, unlike government funders, can be solicited for funding and can have their interest piqued by your communications. Often, as you establish relationships with foundation program officers, you can simply pick up the telephone and ask the program officers to recommend ideas for new projects.

Common Cents

Just remember, never submit a grant proposal to a community foundation unless it is targeted to your own community. Local people endow these foundations and earmark the money to fund local projects.

Organizations outside the headquarters area of national funders like the W. K. Kellogg Foundation, the Pew Charitable Trusts, Gates Foundation, Robert Wood Johnson Foundation, or the Rockefeller Fund only should approach these foundations in response to an RFP or by a special invitation from the funder. An exception can be made for projects that promise to have a national reach or effect. Grants from these foundations are difficult to get without a truly strategic and trendsetting project.

A Checklist of Considerations

You need to consider several things while narrowing your field of prospects:

1. Is your organization a qualified 501(c)(3) nonprofit?
2. What is your organization's program focus, and where does it match funding programs?
3. What type of funding is needed? (See the following table.)
4. How much funding is needed?
5. Why would anyone—particularly a funder—be interested in this project?
6. What kinds of other projects are in progress on that might benefit from a partnership or being merged as part of a "larger picture" of response?

Common Cents

Use systems thinking to resolve difficult social problems. The responses that work best are those in which the entire system mobilizes. It takes businesses, nonprofits, schools, hospitals, communications specialists, community members, and hundreds of others to see the problem—and the potential for change—from every viewpoint.

What Type of Funding Do You Need?

Appropriate for	Government funds	Foundations	Other
Operations	Only as indirect allocation or from local government	Local only	United Way; annual fund drive
Large, costly projects	Yes	Only in partnership	Community members
Small projects	Occasionally	Yes	Internal funding
Capital projects	Rarely	Yes, local only	Community
Model projects	Yes	Yes (include national)	

Appropriate for	Government funds	Foundations	Other
Products/inventions	Yes, sometimes	No	Private investors
Research projects	Yes	Sometimes	By contract
Launch new nonprofit	Rarely	Sometimes	Board members, collaborations
Endowment	No	No	Community
Maintenance endowment	No	As part of capital drive	Community
Sustaining new programs	No	Sometimes	Community

Narrowing the Field of Prospects

Sure, it only costs the stamps to write letters to every foundation or government agency listed in a grant-seeking catalog, but it's a waste of postage and your time if you're unlikely to succeed.

Mass mailings can really damage the credibility of your organization. It's very much like submitting a science-fiction novel to the publisher of Harlequin romances. If they remember your name, they are not likely to read any subsequent submissions that you send in—even if you've written the next bestselling bodice-ripper.

A Better Approach

It's much better to target each letter or grant proposal to the individual interests and focus of each grantmaker. To do that, you have to read the guidelines or the RFP very carefully. When you've discovered several likely prospects, target your submissions to those funders and funding sources that are the most appropriate of all.

Insider Tip

If you are a freelance grant writer, think like a consultant advisor. Your clients will be eager to go after every grant possible. You should advise them when a grant is inappropriate or when their planned approach is not in keeping with the goals of the program.

Don't Make Random Attempts

Maybe you've been successful in garnering large federal grants, but don't start applying for anything and everything. If you see an RFP that you think you could do something with, but the deadline is in two weeks and you haven't even talked to others in the community about partnering, it's best to get some ideas going and start planning now for the next time that RFP is issued.

Read the Guidelines

After the Internet, the second best place to search for appropriate foundations is with a national or regional catalog of foundations. These catalogs are available from publishing houses, your regional association of grantmakers, and the Council on Foundations. Catalogs are often available on CD for interactive keyword searches.

Read the catalog listings carefully, beginning with the focus of the foundation. Often, the catalog has an index of lists by program focus (children, the arts, environment, and so on) that you can use to target the list of appropriate funders for your organization.

Insider Tip

The Foundation Center *(www.foundationcenter.org)* provides an online search engine to identify foundations that might be interested in your project. The Center also hosts the Philanthropy News Digest Message Board *(http://members4.boardhost.com/PNDtalk)*, where you can ask questions of experienced grant writers and fundraisers, share ideas, or reflect on issues associated with fund seeking.

Study the Profile

Next, look at each individual foundation's profile. First, read the purpose of the foundation; you want to make sure they share an interest in your project. You also want to check for hints about the best way to approach them. For instance, a foundation that has interests both in education and in environmental protection might be very interested in a summer-camp program that provides environmental education and experiences for young people.

What's in Their Purpose Statement?

Also, check the purpose statement to make sure that your project exactly fits their program interest. For instance, they might be listed as supporting education, but when you turn to the profile, you learn that their purpose is to strengthen community colleges in their region. Therefore, your program for a local high school is outside their area of interest and not a good fit.

Do They Target a Location?

Next, check for geographic priorities. If the foundation only makes local grants and your agency is on the other side of the state, cross its name off your list. If the foundation makes national grants, your project must have national importance if it is to be considered.

What About Limitations?

Next, look at the restrictions or limitations. Often, a listing contains one of three statements that should be used to eliminate the foundation from your list of prospects. The first two of these statements will say, "Grant funds are generally limited to charitable organizations already favorably known to the foundation," or "Grant funds are committed." Each of these statements means relatively the same thing—that the foundation is already working with established organizations and committing money to those organizations year after year.

The third statement you might see, "No unsolicited proposals considered," means if you can't meet in person with the foundation principals to generate excitement about your proposal before submitting it, you should scratch this foundation from your cold-call list.

Other Restrictions

In addition, most catalog lists of foundations provide a paragraph on what each foundation will not fund. Restricted funding might include some or all of the following:

- Operating support
- Program-related investments/loans
- Endorsements
- Publications
- Conferences/seminars
- Underwriting for special events/sponsorships
- Grants to individuals
- Scholarships
- Fellowships
- Educational loans
- Endowments
- Travel or research grants
- Religious purposes

What Money Is Available?

Finally, look at the range of grants and the typical grant size. This information is published in the catalog, but rarely in guidelines received directly from a foundation. If the grants range from $500 to $10,000 but the typical grant size is $1,000, you will probably approach this funder only when you are at the end of a large fundraising effort or if you have a very small project.

Common Cents

Most foundations prefer not to be the sole funder on a project; they want to see that you are asking others to support the effort, too. Be sure to keep a list of all the foundations from which you are seeking funding and the status of your requests (e.g., pending, not yet requested, committed) both to guide your work and to share with potential funders.

Develop a Strategy

Be strategic in your approach to foundations. Four or five well-targeted grants will serve you and your organization far better than one letter sent to 200 foundations. Expect to be able to narrow the broad field of prospects to about 10 percent. Then work that 10 percent with everything you have.

Reading RFPs

The first thing to read in the RFP is the purpose of the legislation and fund. What does the funder hope to accomplish with its money? If the stated purpose matches the purpose or mission of your program, continue reading. If it somewhat matches, continue reading to see if you can tweak your program to fit more closely. If it's not a fit, move on to the next.

Who Qualifies for Money?

Next, look at the list of qualified applicants. Often the organization qualified to apply is very specific. For instance, some grants call for the applicant to be a community mental-health organization (CMH); others for a local educational agency (LEA); and still others for "330" health clinics, as designated by the federal government.

If your agency doesn't fit the qualification, do not give up! For instance, let's say your organization addresses issues surrounding homelessness. You have a food pantry, free kitchen, a store or outlet for inexpensive clothing, shelter services, work-skill development programs, and substance-abuse programs. Your clientele, however, does not have access to health care, and your organization does not qualify to apply for grants that fund health care for the indigent.

Can You Find a Partner?

In this case, identify the agencies in town that are qualified to provide those services. Call them and suggest a partnership that would enable your organization's clientele to receive free or reduced-cost health care.

What Else to Note

Other important criteria to help you select the right RFP include the following:

- Deadline and amount of narrative required. Let's face it: You are not likely to do a good job on a 300-page grant if the deadline is just two or three weeks off.
- Funding allocation, average amount of awards, and probable number of projects. When the average grant award is several hundred thousand or a million dollars, you can be sure that thousands of qualified organizations will apply. You should calculate the odds of your project being chosen against the number of grants awarded and the time you will commit to writing the proposal.
- Match requirements. Often RFPs are issued for programs that require a certain local match and they will let you know what qualifies as a match.
- Sustainability requirements. Many federal grants require that an organization apply for a three- or four-year decreasing amount grant, in which case the applicant organization must commit to providing increasing amounts of its own money to continue the program over the four-year term of the grant.

Don't be afraid of the long shots. Even when only five grant awards are planned throughout your state, you can help create and "sell" a winning program.

Chapter 6

Letters of Intent and Inquiry

Many people get confused about letters of intent and letters of inquiry. A letter of intent is a form stating that you intend to apply for a grant, and a letter of inquiry is more like a sales pitch, in which you describe your project in the hopes of being invited to submit a complete grant proposal.

Letters of Intent

In a letter of intent, you are telling the granting agency that you plan to respond to a request for proposals. These letters are often sent to governments, since they are the agencies that usually issue RFPs.

Sometimes the granting agency doesn't request a letter of intent at all. If they don't ask for it, don't send one. The agencies that do request letters of intent do so simply to learn how many project proposals they can expect to receive. Sometimes, they might also be interested in finding out from which geographical areas potential proposals will be submitted.

Letters of Inquiry

When you write a letter of inquiry, think of yourself as a sales representative. Your letter of inquiry describes your project and asks for permission to submit a grant proposal. These letters are usually sent to foundation-type funders. Increasingly, foundations are requiring letters of inquiry as the first step in their grant-proposal cycle.

Use a letter of inquiry when the foundation guidelines request this step and/or when you are unclear about whether the foundation funds the type of project you wish to present.

When to Send a Letter of Intent

There are three considerations regarding letters of intent. First, you may not be required to write one at all. Second, you may be requested to write the letter, but not required to send it. Third, you have no choice. In this case, the letter of intent is a necessity, and it will have an absolute deadline for reaching the foundation or government office.

If the instructions say nothing at all about letters of intent, you can assume that it is neither required nor requested. When one is requested but not required, the instructions about a letter of intent say something like, "You are not required to submit a letter of intent, and doing so does not commit you to applying for this grant."

Insider Tip

Only submit a letter of intent when one is requested or required in the RFP. Pay attention to the deadline for submission of the letter; being late is the same as submitting no letter at all. Also, differentiate between required and requested. If you do not submit a required letter of intent by the deadline, you will not be allowed to submit a full proposal for funding.

When a letter of intent is required, the instructions will say something like, "You are required to submit a letter (or notice) of intent to apply by 5:00 P.M. on January 20. Only those organizations submitting a letter of intent by the indicated deadline will be eligible to apply for funds under this grant program." Make no mistake—you must meet that deadline. If it gets there at 5:01 P.M., the letter will be too late.

Components of a Strong Letter of Intent

Letters of intent are short and to the point. They should be no longer than one page, and should contain the following pertinent information:

- Name of grant program
- Number of grant program (if available)

- Name of applicant
- Contact information for applicant
- Category of funding requested (when the RFP has separate categories)

Think of a letter of intent as a form (and in many cases, it actually will be a form), and include little beyond the required information. Don't request additional information or ask questions about your proposal.

Sample Letter of Intent

Increasingly, government agencies that require a letter of intent (or LOI) are supplying forms that you may complete and fax or submit electronically. They look something like this:

NOTICE OF INTENT TO APPLY FOR (2008–09) PROGRAM GRANT

Submit this form no later than January 1, 2008, to assist Department of Education staff in determining the number of reviewers that will be necessary.

Submission of this notice is not a prerequisite for application of grant funds, nor does it obligate the organization to submit an application.

Organization:
Contact Person:
Phone:
Fax:
E-mail:
County(ies) to Be Served:
Mail or fax this form to:
Address:
Fax Number:

Following is a sample notice of intent from a grant seeker.

Dear Name:

The XYZ Nonprofit in City, State, intends to submit a grant proposal in response to program number 123456.9 in the *Federal Register*. Of the three categories for projects described in the designated RFP, XYZ plans to submit under category "C": Nonprofit community collaborations to address shortages of affordable housing.

I understand that this grant proposal will be due by 5:00 P.M. on March 31, year, to your offices. If supplementary information becomes available in the interim or if you have reservations about our qualifications to apply for this grant, please contact me by any of the following means:

Phone: 555-5555
Fax: 555-5566
E-mail: xyz@xyz.com

Thank you.
Sincerely,
Executive Director
XYZ Nonprofit

When to Use a Letter of Inquiry

It is becoming increasingly common for foundations to request a letter of inquiry as the first step in the grant-seeking process. Sometimes, they just want a letter, other times they supply a format you should follow, which is similar to, but shorter than, a full proposal. The rationale behind LOIs is that the foundation really doesn't want you to go to the trouble of completing a long grant proposal if they know it is unlikely to be funded.

A letter of inquiry, unlike a letter of intent, should include a compelling summary of your program plans. Include potential links between your program and the goals of the funder, and, if you are writing the LOI in the form of a letter, request a discussion of the merits of the project.

Components of a Strong Letter of Inquiry

A letter of inquiry should be addressed to a specific person within the granting agency, most often the program officer. If the foundation is not staffed, find the contact person (perhaps a bank official or the founder) in the guidelines. Your letter of inquiry should include the following:

- The problem or need you are addressing
- A summary of the project
- Potential outcomes of the project
- A direct or indirect reference to the ways the project fits the goals or guidelines of the foundation
- An indication of the amount you hope to request and the structure of the grant (i.e., one year, three year, challenge, matching, etc.)
- A brief budget and breakdown of expenses and revenues, including other places the nonprofit has applied or plans to apply for funding
- Reference to partners in the project
- Outcomes of previous fundraising efforts, if any
- A request for a meeting or discussion of the merits of the project and a subsequent invitation to submit a full proposal

Sample Letter of Inquiry

Here is a letter of inquiry one grant writer used when seeking a grant for one of her local nonprofit agencies. Note that she links the project outcomes to the stated objectives of the granting agency found in the RFP's guidelines. Take care to do the same in your letters of inquiry.

Dear Program Officer:

Last fall, the XYZ nonprofit launched a mobile media laboratory, a van equipped with laptop computers, digital video cameras, digital-video editing software, educational software, and e-learning curricula.

The project was deployed in response to needs for technology education and educational enrichment in several areas of the community. In its scheduled visits to inner-city and other public and parochial schools, and community and youth centers, the project provides kindergarten to twelfth-grade enrichment in the subject areas and Internet and video-production training for children and young adults who would otherwise lack access to equipment or connections.

While the educational outcomes for project participants are not yet available, they do appear promising. The project has been enthusiastically received by teachers, students, community members, and organizational representatives. Students have a natural interest in the cameras and computers and quickly learn to operate the equipment and to edit film. Project staff uses that interest to encourage further exploration and study in content-area subjects, as requested by the teaching and administrative staffs of the individual schools.

XYZ now proposes that it use the project not only to enrich academic studies but also to engage children and young adults in the creative process. Through a new program called Project Name, staff plan to assist up to thirty at-risk middle and high school students in exploring their range of talent and in developing the artistic skills needed to support their natural abilities.

Students will participate in the new project five days a week for eight weeks. They will receive several one-act plays written by a local writer, a freelance playwright, and director, who will develop four to six "starter" plays on various topics of interest to young people. He will guide the students in writing the middles and ends to the plays they select. When they are finished, the group will read all the works and select a person to act as the playwright for the remainder of the project. All students will also study stage production, acting, directing, camera operation, and film editing with the playwright and a staff videographer, and through interactive teaching modules on the Internet accessed with project laptops.

Students may then select or try out for assignments related to producing the play and videotaping it as an artistic film. Some will become actors, others set designers, camera operators, costume designers, film editors, etc. Completed plays will be performed live and filmed and edited as short features for broadcast on public-access television or streaming to the Internet. Some components of the plays may be made into performing exhibits for display at the local partner agency. The completed curriculum and resulting work will be shared with other school districts that require new or enhanced arts programs.

Project outcomes include:

- Students will engage in the creative process, learn to work as a group, and come to appreciate their own and others' various talents and skills.
- Students will demonstrate a deeper and long-lasting appreciation for the arts.
- Schools struggling with budgets will have improved, rather than reduced, arts curricula and programming.

XYZ requires $_____$ to launch the project, which will include the following:

- Curriculum development (two months); development of interactive curriculum components and deployment to Web $\$_____$
- Vignettes and 8 weeks' program (five days per week), playwright $\$_____$
- 8 weeks' program, video production and broadcast $\$_____$
- Miscellaneous (costumes, set design, vehicle expenses, etc.) $\$_____$

XYZ is just beginning to explore funding sources for this project. We hope to hear from you soon, not only to learn that you are inviting a full proposal for review by your board, but also to hear your ideas for additional partnerships or program refinements. Thank you for your assistance.

Sincerely,
Executive Director

Some foundations provide LOI forms and guidelines for writing a short narrative. As with grant proposals, follow the instructions and include all the information requested in forms like the sample that follows:

COMMUNITY FOUNDATION
Letter of Inquiry

Legal Name of Organization

Address of Organization

Executive Director/President or CEO   Title

Contact person (if different from CEO/Executive Director)
Phone number

Fax Number   E-mail address

Attachments:

- Does the organization have 501(c)(3) nonprofit status? Yes
  No _____
- Please enclose a copy of the designation letter.
- Please attach a draft project budget.
- Please submit eight copies of your Letter of Inquiry.

     Please use the following format to describe the issue you
hope to address, limiting the description to two additional pages
or less:

- Describe the issue that you hope to address with assistance from
  the Foundation. In what way is your identification of this issue
  and the proposed resolution based on credible data? (Please
  include a summary of the data.)
- Please describe how this project addresses the Foundation's
  principles. If it does not address the principles, it is unlikely to
  be considered.
- How do you propose to address the issue?

- What will be accomplished through this project? How do you plan to evaluate your success?
- What is the proposed time frame for the project?
- Which of the following roles do you foresee the Foundation playing in addressing the identified issue?
  Convening
  Advocating
  Leveraging resources
  Funding (if requesting funds, how much is requested?)
  $_____
  Leading an initiative

  Please do not submit attachments other than those requested.
  $_____ $_____

  Proposed budget for the project

  _____

  Organization's current operating budget

  _____

  Signature of CEO/Executive Director or Board Chairperson
  Date

  Please forward this form, your narrative, and attachments to:
  Community Foundation
  City, State, Zip

Chapter 7

Components of a Grant Proposal

The grant proposal is your response to a request for proposals (RFP) or foundation guidelines. The RFP or guidelines contain your instructions and, most often, an outline of content.

What to Expect

RFPs and guidelines can range from a single sheet to hundreds of pages of instructions and attachments. In nearly every case, the RFP or guidelines require that your proposal include a summary, a needs section, a project description (with goals and objectives), an evaluation section, and a budget.

The entire RFP package is instructional, so it's helpful if you read every word in it. Accomplished grant writers turn first to the outline to determine how much work will go into the proposal. Then they read the remainder of the packet to ensure that they are not missing important information.

Common Cents

Freelance grant writers can use the outline to identify the extent of the work required. Based on the outline, they can determine (a) whether they can schedule adequate time to work on the proposal and (b) the cost estimate for their services.

RFPs from the *Federal Register* are several pages in length. Each page contains up to four columns of very small type. It will probably take approximately one hour to review the contents and make notes on important information that will help guide your writing process.

The outline for the proposal will be apparent, but additional directions may be scattered throughout the RFP. You'll find other important and relevant information such as the following:

- Paper size and composition (The Environmental Protection Agency, for instance, requires use of recycled paper.)
- Spacing (If not specified as double spaced, single space your documents and double space between paragraphs or indent the beginning of each paragraph.)
- Minimum size of typeface (and sometimes the font you must use)
- Deadline for submission (and whether by postmark or arrival date)
- Maximum number of pages
- Address and phone numbers for contact people and for submissions
- Formats
- Qualifications for grantees
- Purpose and goals of the grant program (These are critical, as you want your program to further the goals of the grantor.)
- Necessary forms and attachments
- Instructions for completing forms
- Additional sections required (such as compliance statements, tables of contents, abstracts, etc.)
- Instructions for the order in which you must compile the finished grant-proposal packet (sometimes also provided as a checklist)

Follow the Directions

Always follow the directions. If you forget or ignore directions when you've gone through the instructions, your proposal may not be reviewed. If the instructions have an outline with Roman numerals, numbers, or alpha characters, your response should include the same designations for each section. If you find a section not applicable, you must enter the designation and a header for it before writing, "Not applicable." Grant reviewers use score sheets that are keyed to the instructions, so if your outline doesn't follow theirs or your information is in the wrong place, they may reduce your score.

Review Criteria

Some RFPs replace an outline for your narrative with review criteria or a rubric. Read the questions or qualifications contained in the criteria carefully. Try to determine the gist of each question the grantors are posing. Then respond to each question as completely as you can.

The directions may or may not include review criteria. If they do not, use the questions or headings from the outline to determine exactly how the granting agency wants prospective grantees to answer.

Sample of Need-Section Instructions

Following are instructions, in the form of review criteria, for the need section of an educational grant:

> 1. NEED (Ten points) The proposal provides a brief explanation of why the project is needed. It summarizes the demographics of the district and the selected buildings that will be served by this funding; possible causes for an increase in the number of students requiring special-education services or a decrease in state-assessment reading scores; and the need for new resources and programs for students who are not achieving in reading or who are at risk of reading failure.

Include Relevant Data

In following the instructions, you will provide relevant data, first about the district and then about the building(s) in which you will implement the program. Relevant data in this example would include the number of children and the percentage by building of children failing state assessment and other tests of reading. Other relevant data would point out possible causes for the need.

In addressing the last part of the criteria, you'll want to talk about which programs the buildings have tried in the past and why the programs haven't worked or helped children achieve as much as the principals had hoped. When you complete this section, you'll be set up to begin writing in the project description, addressing why this project will succeed where others have failed.

Follow the Outline

Be sure to follow the outline as closely as you can. Don't write a narrative description of your program—grant proposals are not literature. No matter how good your instincts usually are, if an outline calls for the "need" section to be followed by the description of the program, don't decide that it makes more sense to tell them "what" before you tell them "why."

Insider Tip

Use the same headings the outline does. If they have a heading marked with "B" or Roman numeral "II," make sure that your heading also says "B" or "II." If they give you subheadings marked "a," "b," and "c," create subheadings marked exactly the same way.

The outline is provided to ensure that you address every item on which the proposal will be judged. Following it exactly means that you have responded to all the questions.

What If There Is No Outline?

First of all, don't panic; some RFPs don't come with outlines. The Small Business Innovation and Research (SBIR) grant offered by the federal government through several departments is one of them.

In these cases, request or look up on the Internet previous grant-proposal submissions. Often, the contact person will fax or mail you a copy of a successful proposal and you can use its general outline as a guide for your proposal writing.

A Last Resort

If you cannot locate or acquire a previous submission, base your response on the common elements of a grant proposal or a business plan. Discuss the need or potential market for a product. Describe the project or product. Talk about what remains to be done and how you expect to accomplish it. Develop a budget and explain how you derived the numbers you included. Discuss at length the qualifications of the organization and its staff to carry out the project plan.

Finally, discuss an evaluation of the project or product—what you hope to learn from it and what you'll do with the evaluation once it's complete. Be sure to use headings and subheadings. They will assist readers in navigating the document.

Review Criteria Can Help

Sometimes you'll receive only review criteria without an outline. In these cases, you are expected to follow the review criteria as outlined in the RFP. Summarize the content of each criteria as your headings and subheadings, rather than writing out the entire statement. For instance, the following are review criteria for the first section, "Statement of Need." You may use one or several subheadings within each criterion:

Review Criteria

The extent to which the applicant specifies the goals and objectives of the project and describes how implementation will fulfill the purposes of the Early Learning Opportunities Act (ELOA). The applicant must demonstrate a thorough understanding of the importance of early learning services and activities that help parents, caregivers, and child-care providers incorporate early learning into the daily lives of young children, as well as programs that directly provide early learning to young children.

Suggested Subheadings
Goals and Objectives/Implementation Plan

Review Criteria

The extent to which the applicant demonstrates the need for assistance, including identification and discussion of its needs and resources assessment concerning early learning services. Relevant data from the assessment should be included. Participant and beneficiary information must also be included.

Suggested Subheadings
Need for Assistance/Target Population

Review Criteria

The extent to which the applicant describes its resources assessment and the relevance of the results as the basis for determining its objectives and need for assistance.

Suggested Subheadings
Needs Assessment

Review Criteria

The extent to which the applicant demonstrates how it will give preference to supporting activities/projects that maximize the use of resources through collaboration with other early learning programs, provide continuity of services for young children across the age spectrum, and help parents and other caregivers promote early learning with their young children. The applicant must provide information about how decisions will be made about who will provide each early learning service and/or activity funded through this grant.

Suggested Subheadings
Partners and Their Roles/Maximizing Resources

Review Criteria

The extent to which the applicant demonstrates that it has worked with local education agencies to identify cognitive, social, emotional, and motor-developmental abilities that are necessary to support children's readiness for school; that the programs, services, and activities assisted under this title will represent developmentally appropriate steps toward the acquisition of those abilities; and that the programs, services, and assisted activities provide benefits for children cared for in their own homes as well as children placed in the care of others.

Suggested Subheadings

Review of Literature/Lessons Learned

Essential Components

A good grant proposal, like a good news story, tells who, what, where, when, why, and how.

"Who" is both the organization you are describing and the target population whose needs you expect to address with your project. You'll answer that in the Need Section of the proposal.

"Where" is a description of the city or region in which the project will take place. You have to address where in the Needs Section.

"What" describes your project in detail. You'll place this in the Project Description.

"When" is your timeline of activities and it is contained in the Project Description.

"How" and *"Why?"* You'll be answering these in various places throughout the RFP, like so:

- How many (people, units of service, hours)?
- How much (change is expected in the population/environment/outcomes)?
- How will you know? (evaluation)
- How much does it cost? (budget)
- How does your program fit the goals of the grant program?
- Why did you choose this particular program?
- Why is your organization the best one to do the work?
- Why do you think the project will work?
- Why should the grantor care?

You will be asked to describe all the essential components listed here in every grant proposal. Some RFPs, however, will also ask such things as the history of the organization, the genesis for the project, the roles of partners in the project, and the input by constituents or the target population into the design or evaluation of the project.

You might be asked to include your plan for disseminating the results of your evaluation. Some agencies want to know what literature you used in developing your project. You'll also be asked how you will sustain the program after grant funds are expended.

Insider Tip

A new trend in grant proposals, especially among foundations, is a question about constituent input into program design and/or the evaluation process. This is to help nonprofit-organization staff begin to realize that they are not the final arbiters of someone else's need.

Federal Register Instructions Example

The sample RFP shown here is one of the tougher ones, in part because the language of the RFP is that of experts. We suggest that only those who are experts in the field of child care attempt this grant proposal as a first project.

20527 FEDERAL REGISTER / VOL. 67, NO. 80 / THURSDAY, APRIL 25, 2002 / NOTICES

Part III General Instructions for Preparing the Uniform Project Description

ACF is particularly interested in specific factual information and statements of measurable goals in quantitative terms. Project descriptions are evaluated on the basis of substance, not length. Extensive exhibits are not required. Cross-referencing should be used rather than repetition. Supporting information concerning activities that will not be directly funded by the grant or information that does not directly pertain to an integral part of the grant-funded activity should be placed in an appendix.

The Project Description Overview Purpose

The project description provides a major means by which an application is evaluated and ranked to compete with other applications for available assistance. The project description should be concise and complete and should address the activity for which federal funds are being requested. Supporting documents should be included where they can present information clearly and succinctly. In preparing your project description, all information requested through each specific evaluation criteria should be provided. Awarding offices use this and other information in making their funding recommendations. It is important, therefore, that this information be included in the application. Pages should be numbered, and a table of contents should be included for easy reference.

A. Project Summary/Abstract/Geographic Location

Provide a summary of the project description (a page or less) with reference to the funding request. Describe the precise location of the project and boundaries of the area to be served by the proposed project. Maps or other graphic aids may be attached.

B. Objectives and Need for Assistance

Clearly identify the physical, economic, social, financial, institutional, and/or other problem(s) requiring a solution. The need for assistance must be demonstrated, and the principal and subordinate objectives of the project must be clearly stated; supporting documentation, such as letters of support and testimonials from concerned interests other than the applicant, may be included.

Any relevant data based on planning studies should be included or referred to in the endnotes/footnotes. Incorporate demographic data and participant/beneficiary information, as needed. In developing the project description, the applicant may volunteer or be requested to provide information on the total range of projects currently being conducted and supported (or to be initiated), some of which may be outside the scope of the program announcement.

C. Results or Benefits Expected

Identify the results and benefits to be derived. For example, specify the number of children and families to be served and how the services to be provided will be funded consistent with the local needs assessment. Or, explain how the expected results will benefit the population to be served in meeting its needs for early learning services and activities.

D. Approach/Evaluation Approach

Outline a plan of action that describes the scope and detail of how the proposed work will be accomplished. Account for all functions or activities identified in the application. Cite factors that might accelerate or decelerate the work and state your reason for taking the proposed approach rather than others.

Describe any unusual features of the project such as design or technological innovations, reductions in cost or time, or extraordinary social and community involvement.

Provide quantitative monthly or quarterly projections of the accomplishments to be achieved for each function or activity in such terms as the number of people to be served and the number of activities accomplished. When accomplishments cannot be quantified by activity or function, list them in chronological order to show the schedule of accomplishments and their target dates.

If any data is to be collected, maintained, and/or disseminated, clearance may be required from the U.S. Office of Management and Budget (OMB). This clearance pertains to any "collection of information that is conducted or sponsored by ACF."

List organizations, cooperating entities, consultants, or other key individuals who will work on the project, along with a short description of the nature of their effort or contribution.

E. Evaluation

Provide a narrative addressing how the results of the project and the conduct of the project will be evaluated. In addressing the evaluation of results, state how you will determine the extent to which the project has achieved its stated objectives and the extent to which the accomplishment of objectives can be attributed to the project. Discuss the criteria to be used to evaluate results, and explain the methodology that will be used to determine whether the needs identified and discussed are being met, and whether the project results and benefits are being achieved. With respect to the conduct of the project, define the procedures to be employed to determine whether the project is being conducted in a manner consistent with the work plan presented, and discuss the impact of the project's various activities on the project's effectiveness.

F. Additional Information

The following are requests for additional information that need to be included in the application:

Staff and Position Data: Provide a biographical sketch for each key person appointed and a job description for each vacant key position. A biographical sketch will also be required for new key staff as appointed.

Plan for Continuance Beyond Grant Support: Provide a plan for securing resources and continuing project activities after federal assistance has ceased.

Organizational Profiles: Provide information on the applicant organization(s) and cooperating partners, such as organizational charts, financial statements, audit reports or statements from CPA/licensed public accountants, employer identification numbers, names of bond carriers, contact persons and telephone numbers, child-care licenses, and other documentation of professional accreditation, information on compliance with federal/state/local government standards, documentation of experience in the program area, and other pertinent information. Any nonprofit organization submitting an application must submit proof of its nonprofit status in its application at the time of submission. The nonprofit agency can accomplish this by providing a copy of the applicant's listing in the Internal Revenue Service's (IRS) most recent list of tax-exempt organizations described in section 501(c)(3) of the IRS code, or by providing a copy of the currently valid IRS tax-exemption certificate, or by providing a copy of the articles of incorporation bearing the seal of the state in which the corporation or association is domiciled.

Third-Party Agreements: Include written agreements between grantees and subgrantees or subcontractors or other cooperating entities. These agreements must detail scope of work to be performed, work schedules, remuneration, and other terms and conditions that structure or define the relationship.

Letters of Support: Provide statements from community, public, and commercial leaders that support the project proposed for funding. All submissions should be included in the application OR by application deadline.

G. Budget and Budget Justification

Provide line-item detail and detailed calculations for each budget-object class identified on the Budget Information form. Detailed calculations must include estimation methods, quantities, unit costs, and other similar quantitative detail sufficient for the calculation to be duplicated. The detailed budget must also include a breakout by the funding sources identified in Block 15 of the SF–424.

Provide a narrative budget justification that describes how the categorical costs are derived. Discuss the necessity, reasonableness, and allocation of the proposed costs.

Chapter 8

Preparing to Write

Always review the guidelines or RFP closely before you begin writing the first draft. Learn as much as you can about your audience—are they foundation trustees and staff or volunteers who may be your peers? Read between the lines of the RFP or guidelines to help you determine what they need and want to know about your organization and its programs. Focus on their interests rather than on what you need or want to tell them, and you're on your way to writing a successful grant proposal.

Know Your Readers

The first rule of all good writing is to know—and understand—your audience. How much do they already know about the subject? How much do they want to learn from your document? What are their biases? What are their interests? For your purposes, there are two different kinds of grant readers: one reads foundation proposals, the other, government responses to RFPs.

Foundation Readers

Foundation staff, and occasionally, trustees, read foundation grant proposals. It helps, therefore, to read the guidelines, annual reports, or Web information thoroughly to learn as much as you can about their personal and collective interests before you submit a proposal.

Often, you can go to the local foundation to meet staff and discuss your proposal. Then you can revise it before they present it to their trustees. Alternately, program officers may come to your office (called a "site visit"), or ask you to meet in theirs so they can get more information to share with their trustees and to support their recommendations regarding funding.

These program officers are the critical people to impress in the foundation grant-seeking process. Listen to all of their requests for additional information and respond in a timely manner. If they want you to rewrite an entire proposal, do so. They are not the enemy; they know their boards and what the members want covered in proposals. Their job is to go before the trustees with solid reasons for recommending funding or declining the proposals—give them the tools to help you.

Government Grant Readers

In the case of government grants, the proposal readers are the decision-makers or judges for each proposal. They are the most important figures in the entire process. They award points for each section, total the points, and average them with the scores of the other readers to come up with a final score. That final score must total an established number for the project to be funded. Recommendations of the judges don't have to be supported by the reviewers or questioned by the funding agency.

In most cases, these proposal readers are experts in their fields and have responded to a call for readers or been recruited by the issuing department. Proposal readers often represent a cross-section of geography, expertise, and interests, and are usually peers of those who are submitting proposals.

Common Cents

Very often, RFPs will include a supplementary call for readers. That means that any person who receives the RFP may also apply to become a judge. If the reader also represents an agency that has applied for the grant, he or she will not be assigned to review his or her own organization's proposal.

A Tight Timeline for Readers

Proposal reviews usually take place in less than a week. Readers are sent ten or more proposals to read and score and return to the funding agency for final tallying. Usually, each proposal has three to five judges. Reviewers are provided score sheets to guide their judging, often in the form of rubrics or review criteria identical to that provided in the RFP, and a cover sheet or space to write comments. While they are not required to justify their scoring, they often do provide comments that you can use later to strengthen a failed proposal.

Scoring an RFP

While grant proposals are competitive, the individual proposals are not judged one against another. The final score is the average of all scores awarded by all readers of that proposal. That is the only criterion upon which funding is based, except in cases where the funding agency further ensures geographic equity.

A high score, however, does not always guarantee funding. If, for instance, 1,000 proposals are submitted and 500 of them score 90 out of 100 points, the benchmark for funding will be raised—to 95 or higher. If the grant has limited funds, it means that the grantmaker will fund only the best of the best projects, not all of the good projects.

Insider Tip

As used in RFPs, a rubric is a chart that contains various classifications and explanations and the range of points that may be awarded to each category in the grant proposal. The readers of proposals use the rubric to guide their awarding of points to each section of your proposal. It is provided to grant writers to help them ensure that their responses to each section are as comprehensive as possible.

In the case of government grants, it is important to remember that you are writing to your peers or, in the case of freelance grant writers, to the peers of your clients. If your clients understand and support the narrative, chances are that the judges will be equally impressed.

Outlining

Outlining a grant proposal is the easiest thing you have to do. Simply follow the outline provided in the RFP or guidelines exactly.

Every Roman numeral in the RFP should have a corresponding Roman numeral in your outline. The same is true for all alpha characters and numbers. You also may want to include the point value for each question or some of your notes to the outline. You can delete them later.

Brainstorming

Once you have an outline and questions, sit down with other members of your organization and potential collaborators to brainstorm ideas for the program. This is not your typical brainstorming session in which "anything goes."

For this session, you should lay out the program mandates from the grant on one page of a flip chart and the components of programs your organization currently has in place on another page. Begin by comparing the two to see how you can modify existing programs to fit more closely with the program sought in the RFP.

If there is information that you aren't sure of, or areas you know less about, ask other staff members for their assistance so you can make sure you have the most complete data possible.

Common Cents

If you're working as a freelancer, schedule a meeting with your clients to gather information. Provide feedback to clarify with comments such as, "I hear you saying that the program should focus on 'a' rather than 'b,' is that right?" Don't end the meeting until you feel you have enough information to write a solid first draft.

Your brainstorming group can and should become your grant-seeking team. You'll need help with many of tasks throughout the writing process; often, one or two members of the team can give you a hand. If you're freelancing, make it clear to team members that the more they help, the fewer hours you will have to spend on non-writing tasks and the lower your final invoice for services will be.

Tasks you can assign the team members include the following:

- Calling other organizations for data
- Locating internal data
- Developing budgets and moving draft budgets through internal approval channels
- Reviewing drafts
- Locating library resources if needed
- Providing anecdotal evidence of need

Planning Responsive Programs
You are the person most familiar with the requirements outlined in the RFP, and as you gain experience writing grants, you will become very familiar with what local foundations will and will not fund. You'll be able to use this knowledge to guide you as you help develop programs and new ideas for collaborations with other groups.

A Federal Grant RFP Sample
Now let's look at a federal grant RFP. In this case, you must follow all the criteria exactly in planning your program and ensuring that it provides each and every service described.

According to the guidelines, the purposes of the grant program are:

1. To increase the availability of voluntary programs, services, and activities that support early childhood development, increase parent effectiveness, and promote the learning readiness of

young children so that young children enter school ready to learn

2. To support parents, childcare providers, and caregivers who want to incorporate early learning activities into the daily lives of young children

3. To remove barriers to the provision of an accessible system of early childhood learning programs in communities throughout the United States

4. To increase the availability and affordability of professional development activities and compensation for caregivers and child-care providers

5. To facilitate the development of community-based systems of collaborative service-delivery models characterized by resource sharing, linkages between appropriate supports, and local planning for services

What to Do

List each of the criteria on a large flip-chart sheet and post them in the room during your team's brainstorming session. Have members respond to ways in which the proposed project already answers these requirements. Then have the team suggest ways that they could strengthen the program to ensure that it meets all the criteria to the highest degree possible.

What's the Deadline?

Plan backward from the deadline. The closer the deadline, the more you should call on your team to assist you. Work backward from the shipping date, not the deadline for arrival at the grantor's office, unless it's a local office where you can drop off the proposal.

Your schedule must include:

*   Meetings
*   Time to write at least two drafts

- Draft-review times for team members
- Time to complete forms and get signatures
- Time to get and, sometimes, write support letters
- Time for gathering attachments and copying and collating

A typical schedule that a grantwriter would provide a client looks like this:

Date	Process/activity	Responsibility
2/2	Complete draft 1 with questions and blanks for first review	writer
2/6–2/9	Return draft with suggestions for revisions	team
	Meet to discuss issues/questions	team and writer
Week of 2/9	Revise draft	writer
	Begin preliminary budget	team
Week of 2/16	Review draft 2	team
	Meet to discuss attachments, narrative, potential list of support letters, etc.	team and writer
Week of 2/23	Revise draft	writer
	Request support letters, locate additional attachments	team
	Finalize budget	team and writer
3/2	Finalize draft and attachments and submit for approval	writer
3/6	Compile completed narrative for final review, page allowance, attachments, and forms	writer
3/6–3/9	Outstanding forms, signatures, letters, etc.	writer and team
3/10	Ship date for arrival by 3/11	writer

A Checklist of Procedures and Tasks

The following tasks will become second nature as you write more and more grant proposals. Here are some of the things you must be sure to accomplish prior to writing:

1. Outline the grant following the outline of the RFP/guidelines.
2. Brainstorm and list potential collaborations.
3. Contact potential collaborators to participate in project-design meetings.
4. Develop a calendar of draft submissions and reviews with anyone who has agreed to review the proposal.
5. Develop a list of outstanding documents. Establish who or where these documents will come from.
6. Write letters of support, send them to signers, and set a deadline for return of signed originals.
7. Set up a file folder with separate sections for narrative drafts, forms, original letters and attachments, RFP/guidelines, and background materials.
8. Make a list of data required and potential sources for data. Include phone numbers and contact names in case you can assign this job to a grant-seeking team member.

Chapter 9

Planning for Letters of Support

Experienced grant writers will tell you that it's essential to plan ahead for your letters of support. You must identify and contact people, and sometimes even write their letters of support! Address this early in the process to ensure that all the letters arrive in time to be sent with your grant package.

What Is a Letter of Support?

There are generally two types of letters of support. One is from an organization that is a partner to the project. Recently, this type of letter has been supplemented or replaced with a formal partnership agreement, which is required by some grantmakers.

Common Cents

If another nonprofit organization is partnering with yours to deliver services, that organization must put its commitment to the project in writing either through a letter of support or an interagency agreement. Never submit a grant proposal from a partnership without written agreements between the partners for how the project will be implemented and how grant funds will be expended.

The second type comes from community leaders, program collaborators, or organizational-service recipients. These letters of support validate the need for the program. In addition to providing support for the proposing agency and/or its program, they may also indicate ways in which others in the community are willing to support the project.

Who Should Write It and Sign It?

The letter of support can be written by anyone. Since the grant writer is most familiar with the program and what has already been stated in the narrative, he or she often writes this letter. The letter must, however, be signed by the head of the supporting organization. It also must be printed on that organization's letterhead and supplied as an original document; you may not rely on faxed copies. Therefore, you must make certain that the originals arrive at your office in time for you to attach them to the proposal. Your best bet is to take charge early in the process.

Insider Tip

Because everyone wants to see fellow organizations secure grants and because since government grants return tax revenue to their community, it is often easy to get fellow organizations to agree to write letters of support. It is, however, far more difficult to get people to follow up on their commitments. You'll need to follow up, seek new support if necessary, or offer to write it for them.

If you do write all the letters of support as a service to your client or employer, make sure all of the letters are different. The best way to do that is to interview the agencies involved. That way you can learn unique things about each one and incorporate that information into the letter.

When to Start Soliciting Letters

As soon as you know how many collaborators you'll have on the project, start soliciting their letters of support. If you are writing them, you should e-mail your final draft copy to them so they can print it on the organization's letterhead.

As you develop your schedule for completing the grant, add in a check-back point for those agencies that have agreed to write a letter of support but have not yet sent it in. Request that they send their original letters by mail or courier directly to you or to your client's office—and stress that the letters should be unfolded and sent in a large envelope. Your other option is to pick them up from each agency.

Writing a Support Letter

You don't want the judges to read, "This is a great project, so please fund it." Letters must be specific so that it's clear to the reader exactly what the organization is supporting. For instance, is the letter-writing organization providing some sort of collaborative service to the project? Is it supporting the need statement and stating that its own constituents would take advantage of the proposed project? Is the letter a letter of agreement to jointly provide services? Or is it a letter from a leader in the community who is vouching for the organization's track record?

Common Cents

Letters of support should not be generic. Encourage your writers to state their commitments specifically. Provide them information or a draft proposal so they can link their commitments to those made in the proposal. Or, if that fails, write the support letter and ask that the author of record review it, print it on his or her organizational letterhead, and sign it.

Support letters must state the fundamental components of the program that the letter writer is supporting so that the reader knows the agency is familiar with the project and knows exactly what the agency is committing to doing.

Sample Support Letters

The following examples show four different types of support letters. Each has a different function. In the first letter, the proposing agency and its primary partners signed the same letter and asked those affected by the program to sign in support of the project:

Date

We, the undersigned, understand that the XYZ project requires a strong network of caring individuals and service providers if it is to help create systemic change, improve the XXX community, and serve as a model of effective practices for reducing prostitution and its resulting social problems. We, therefore, commit ourselves and the organizations and agencies we represent to building and strengthening that network, to participating in the XYZ Advisory Committee, and to providing services judged important to helping prostitutes rebuild their lives.

Sincerely,

Chief of Police Department   *University School of Social Work*
Neighborhood Association   *Social Work Agency*

The second sample letter supports a need for services proposed by one agency and states that a local school district would take advantage of such services if they were available. You can tell that the author of the letter has clearly read the proposal and knows what the grant writer has said about the school district and the planned project. She affirms the need for the project in the school district and links program outcomes to the district's students' outcomes.

Date

Dear name:

On behalf of XXX Public Schools and our students, I strongly support the Mobile Media Laboratories planned for launch by the XYZ Nonprofit Organization in Fall, 2007. As you already know, our students come from families that range from wealthy to indigent. At one of our ten elementary schools, more than 90 percent of students participate in the Federal Free/Reduced Lunch program; at another, only 22 percent participate. The Mobile Media Lab will help us "level the playing field" particularly for students who don't have access to home computers, high-speed Internet connections, or digital video cameras.

Every graduate of XXX Schools must meet our exit standards, which mandate that students are effective communicators (expressing and listening), personal managers, quality producers, global citizens, critical/creative thinkers, and self-directed learners. Our job is to provide the resources that help students meet these standards and to modify those tools as students, culture, and future worker requirements change. The Mobile Media Lab will assist us greatly in providing tools that will help our students gather and analyze information, make informed decisions, engage in creative communications, and explore new vehicles for teaching and learning.

The opportunity to link, through the lab's wireless connections, with XYZ's television and radio stations or directly to the web, is sure to generate excitement among our students. Media can be a strong motivator for more reluctant scholars, and broadcasting is sure to help some of our students overcome shyness and improve their self-esteem.

We look forward to working with you and participating in an ongoing evaluation of the Mobile Media Lab and its programs.

Sincerely,

Assistant Superintendent for Curriculum and Instruction

The third letter comes from a community leader in support of a local agency. In this case, the author is president of a local foundation and is familiar with the work of the proposing nonprofit. A letter from a community leader or fellow funder has greater importance when sent to a foundation in the state or region; in other words, peer to peer. Such a letter would not be as necessary to a federal grant project.

Date

Dear name:

I strongly encourage the City Foundation to consider XYZ's grant application for improvements to the structure and programming at the Youth Center.

This program is critical to preventing juvenile delinquency and building the self-esteem of inner-city youth in our community. When it was conceived nearly sixty years ago, it was the first in the nation to utilize police officers in the roles of mentors to at-risk youngsters; it remains a model for other communities in the nation for its success, longevity, and unique niche in meeting the needs of young people.

The XXX Foundation, one of the state's largest family foundations, has supported programming at the center despite the fact that the foundation does not generally support programs for teens, but rather, focuses its charitable giving on programs that provide early childhood development. This support is testament to XYZ's importance to prevention services in our community.

If I can answer any questions or provide additional information, please do not hesitate to contact me.

Sincerely,

Foundation President
XXX Foundation

The fourth sample is really two samples in one. The letters were required by the federal government and are, in essence, an agreement to partner on the project proposed.

Date

Dear name:

The process of grant-proposal development is often beneficial, and the FAST opportunity has proved to be perhaps the most beneficial development process ever. As a result of discussions about our various programs, efforts, and goals, the state Small Business Development Center (SBDC) and the state Economic Development Corporation (EDC) have joined in partnership to focus on commercializing technologies developed by state-based entrepreneurs.

The state SBDC will continue to work one on one with potential and current small-business owners, and, with four new staff members, will intensify its efforts and expand its support network for technology innovators. The support network for technology innovators is automatically strengthened by the partnership with the state EDC, which has initiated the state Life Science Corridor, the Emerging Technology Challenge Fund, Smart Zones, and Venture Quest, among its other efforts to strengthen our state's place in the "new economy."

The SBDC operates from twelve regional offices and thirty-one satellite offices throughout the state, each of which is affiliated with a regional college or university. Four technology-resources counselors (two hired by the state SBDC and two hired from grant funds, if we are successful) will cover the entire state, working closely with regional directors, small-business counselors, and innovators to deliver the right combination of services needed to develop and commercialize innovative technologies.

We look forward to our working partnership with the state EDC, as we believe this is the best way to identify, reach, and support technology innovators and, ultimately, to bring life-enhancing and, sometimes, life-saving innovations to people who will benefit from them.

Sincerely,

State Director

Date

Dear name:

The state Economic Development Corporation (EDC) is proud to announce its newly created working partnership with the state Small Business Development Center (SBDC)—a strong addition to the statewide network of initiatives already launched in support of technology innovation and economic development in our state.

The state's economic development entity, the EDC, has developed several entrepreneurial initiatives, including the state Life Science Corridor, the Emerging Technology Challenge Fund, Smart Zones, Venture Quest, and a number of venture- and angel-capital-formation activities, as well as support for SBIR/STTR and other R&D grant seeking.

While we have undertaken creation of this large, statewide support system, we have not had a great deal of one-on-one experience with technology innovators. The partnership with the state SBDC allows us to deploy responses and resources individualized to the needs of each technology innovator.

The two organizations share a goal for commercializing technology innovations and securing the state's place in the "new economy." We are excited about this emerging partnership and its many possibilities.

Thank you for your review of our enclosed grant application. We look forward to your response.

Sincerely,

State EDC President

Knowing How Many Letters You Need

You must have letters of support from every formal partner and every organization highlighted as a collaborator in the grant-proposal narrative; it sends up red flags if they are not included.

Insider Tip

Some letters of support are really partnership agreements and are required by the grantor. Make sure that, if you compose these letters, you outline the scope of work for both partners and that both partners read, understand, and agree to the division of responsibilities, their roles in the partnership, and the dispersal of grant funds.

It's also a good idea to provide as many letters as you can that support the case for need for the service you are proposing. Letters of support from leadership agencies and individuals are simply "icing" and can be attached or not, as you see fit.

Be sure to check the instructions for page limits on attachments. Select from the very best and most critical support letters if you have a limit. Also encourage all support-letter writers to keep their missives to one page only.

Chapter 10

Writing a Statement of Need

Usually, the first section of a grant proposal, the statement of need—also called a "case statement" or a "problem statement"—is your chance to introduce your organization and community to the proposal judges. Most often, federal grants are awarded to communities where the need is greatest. In the case of foundations, grants are most often successful when they clearly outline a social or community problem and propose a creative, workable solution. Either audience needs strong data to support the problem or need statement.

Introduce the Organization

In many foundation guidelines, information about your organization comes last in the outline, and the directions in a federal grant RFP usually don't have a section in which you can introduce your organization. So the best place to tell them who you are and what you do is in the needs statement. Not only is the needs statement most often the first section of the proposal, it's also where you will describe your community and your target population. Use this section to "set the stage" so that readers of the proposal begin to visualize how and why your proposed program will work.

Use data to introduce your organization. Tell the reader how many people you serve, what percentage of the population you reach, how many more people there are that you need to target for services, and any other numbers that help you introduce the organization and state the need for funding its services.

Selecting Appropriate Data

Data is the evidence you present to make your case. Find supporting data from your organization and other nonprofit agencies in your community. Just as in a court case, you must present irrefutable evidence of the need for action, and thus, funding.

The RFP will describe some necessary data, but you must be the judge of what other data you can gather to support your case. Some of the more unusual data grantwriters have been asked to supply include the following:

- Rate of suicide or suicide attempts among high school students
- Blood lead levels among children living in a specific area of the city
- Purchase date of every piece of computer equipment in a building
- Number of individuals in the United States who use a prosthetic arm or leg
- Infant mortality rate by ethnicity, age of mother, family income, and native language of mother
- Number of active prostitutes in a city

You will be asked to supply numbers to support your case and to form your evaluation of the program. Along with being a good writer, you will have to develop your research and mathematics skills. First you have to find the data and then you have to "crunch the numbers." For instance, you will often be given raw numbers when the RFP requests percentages or vice versa.

Locating Data

Locating appropriate data can be difficult. Census data are helpful, but often they are not current or specific enough to support an emerging need. When a community has a low unemployment rate during the year of the census, for example, but then unemployment rates steadily rise over the next several years, census data can actually harm your case for a job-training program. While your local United Way may collect the data, they often must rely on information provided by member organizations, and generally the United Way does not verify those numbers.

Best Sources for Data

Individual and specific organizations are generally the best source for reliable data. For instance, if you need to know how many students participate in the federal lunch program in a school district, you simply have to call the central district office to find out. Call the police department for crime statistics; the juvenile court for teen delinquency rates; or the YWCA for domestic-abuse cases.

Sometimes you'll just have to estimate. In those cases, tell the reader how you arrived at your estimate. For instance, to determine the number of prostitutes in a city, first find out the number of men and women arrested for prostitution. Go over the list with the police officers who cover the area where prostitutes are known to hang out. They will tell you which of the arrests are repeat offenders and will also provide you a more accurate estimate than the arrest numbers indicate. You'd write something like, "In 2002, the police made more than 300 arrests of approximately 280 women and twenty men. Officers working with the population estimate that the number of active prostitutes on city streets and in known houses of prostitution is between 500 and 700 people."

Insider Tip

Another good source of data can be a local or nearby university. Telephone the social sciences department and ask to speak to a researcher. Some really helpful university departments will assign graduate students to help you update old data or extrapolate pieces of data from aggregates.

Clip Published Reports

You can also clip newspaper articles that you encounter throughout the year that may be related to the people your organization reaches. The reporter has already gathered the data to support his or her article, so you can just clip the information and file it in a notebook, saving it for later so you have a source to go to the next time you need data for a grant proposal.

Use Data to Support Your Case

It's not enough just to put the data requested in the RFP. Your next step is to use it well so that you can demonstrate that your community needs the particular service or program your organization is proposing.

Analyze why the RFP has asked for certain information and how relevant the data that you've gathered are to your program. For instance, you may have the data on teens who have attempted suicide, but do you use it to justify a case for additional computers in the schools? Typically, you would use that data in grants about something like health or mental-health services in the schools, but there are exceptions.

State Your Case

You must pull all the data together to form a picture of the situation and to set the stage for your proposed program. Make sure that the data support the program you are proposing. If you tell the reviewers, for instance, that 90 percent of prostitutes are drug abusers, then you should have a drug-abuse treatment or intervention program in your overall program.

Be coherent. This is where you lay a foundation for understanding why you selected the program you are now proposing. As with the foundation of a building, if you don't make a strong case here, everything you add later is in danger of collapse.

Use a Gap Analysis

When you don't have a lot of data to support your need statement, you can pull together a team of people who are collaborating on the grant and have them help you perform a gap analysis.

A gap analysis is a means to identify hindrances or other roadblocks that might otherwise prevent you from achieving a desired goal. It forces a realistic look at the current situation and helps identify the things that need to be done to arrive at the desired future/goals. Use your data (the present state of affairs), your outcomes (the desired future), and the gaps between them (the need). Following is a step-by-step method for a gap analysis.

Identify the Future State

Where do you want to be? What's the desired outcome? Add detail to your goal statement. List the information and thoughts and details in a box labeled "Desired Future."

Identify the Present State

How are things now? Describe the same components featured in the future state, but do so in present terms. For instance, state that you know that 90 percent of prostitutes are drug users. You know that approximately 2 percent of prostitutes are male transvestites. And you know that there are gay male prostitutes but that they are not on the street and you have no way of counting them or analyzing the extent of the problem. Again, be very detailed. Post the ideas generated in a box labeled "Present State."

Focus on the Gaps

Ask teammates and collaborators to talk through the following points:

What are the gaps?

What are the barriers to achieving the goals?

What's missing in already-existing services?

Write a Needs Statement

Use the results of the gaps you focused on to assist in writing your needs statement. In the above example, the organization found that there were no services that addressed the need for childcare while prostitutes were in drug rehabilitation. Although they had other data, they were more interested in addressing the greatest barrier they found, that relating to prostitutes seeking drug-rehabilitation services.

Citing Resources

While you don't have to cite every source of data or create a research paper with bibliography and footnotes, it is important to cite any experts you quote and to credit published reports from which you take data. Add just a few resources and citations if they are available. For example, if you are writing about prostitution in your city, add some statistics about prostitution in general.

> *Nationally, police departments are estimated to spend approximately 40 percent of their budgets on enforcing prostitution laws. It is time-consuming police work, requiring in many cases that officers pair up, obtain a solicitation form, and make an arrest of a suspected prostitute. Then they have to transport the woman or man to the police station or jail, complete fingerprinting and identification, write and file a report, and testify in court. Teams of police officers in other cities are estimated to spend twenty-one officer hours on each prostitution arrest. ("Prostitution Control Costs," Hastings Law Journal, April, 1987.)*

Be sure when you cite national statistics to link them to the case in your own community. In the above example, you might say: "Here in City, State, the police department receives no special budget allocation for battling prostitution. Instead, it works with courts, social-service agencies, and others to share and reduce costs. It has also streamlined the arrest process to reduce the amount of time officers spend completing paperwork. Last year's 300 arrests cost the city only $10,000 (after fines were paid); police officers spent approximately fourteen hours per arrest."

Sample Needs Statement

Use the first paragraph of the sample needs statement to introduce the organization and the community it serves.

City Public Schools (CPS) is a public school system serving nearly 6,000 children and young adults in kindergarten through twelfth grades, alternative education, preschool, and adult-education programs. The district is composed of portions of the cities of City A, City B, and of Township C. CPS includes eight elementary, two middle, one alternative, one alternative charter, and two high school buildings.

The predominant service area is the city of City A, which was built as a suburb of City just after World War II and was composed primarily of "tract" housing modeled after Levittown, New York, developments. Although City A now has more diverse housing options, some industry, and much retail, according to experts on land-use trends, it is becoming increasingly poorer as upwardly mobile families move to more distant suburbs. Whereas in 1970, city residents earned exactly the average regional median income, by 1990, they earned only 87 percent of the regional median income. This decline is indicated in the City Public Schools as the number of children participating in the federal free/reduced lunch program has increased from approximately 10 percent in 1970 to 26 percent in the 1996–97 school year and to more than 29 percent in 1998–99.

Nevertheless, the City community has a history of supporting educational institutions and initiatives. Although many communities of comparable size have only one high school, City voters have continually approved school-support millages and bond issues that enable support of two high schools of 700–900 students, which Carnegie Institute researchers have found to be the most appropriate size for learning. One elementary school has garnered national attention for its experimentation with a longer school year and nearly 100-percent parental involvement. Parent participation at CPS elementary school conferences regularly exceeds 95 percent.

The community has also supported increased technology resources and learning opportunities for its children. In 1992 and 1997, the CPS community passed two bond issues for a combined total of $57 million ($14 and $43 million respectively). These bonds were used to provide computer connectivity (LAN/WAN network) in and across all CPS educational and support buildings, to purchase computer hardware, and to remodel, repair, and add to existing school buildings. Today, each school building has a twenty-five-station networked computer lab in its media center. One elementary school has an additional three to five computers in each classroom. The two middle schools have a second lab in addition to the one in the media center, and the two high schools have two labs in addition to the computers in their media centers.

Community support has enabled CPS to score "high-tech" on the STaR (Standardized Testing and Reporting) chart in the areas of connectivity and hardware. Computer-to-student ratios in buildings ranges from twelve-to-one in Elementary 1 to four-to-one in Elementary 2. The eight CPS elementary schools serve nearly 2,600 students (K–5) with approximately 370 computers. The combined ratio of students to computers in the elementary schools is seven-to-one.

To date, the hardware and connectivity have improved only the technological "look" of CPS schools, but they have failed to improve learning as measured on standardized tests. In fact, in all but a very few instances, test scores among CPS elementary students, despite additional tutorial resources and testing strategies, fell dramatically between the 1996–97 and 1997–98 school years.

The following chart indicates the percentage of CPS elementary students scoring satisfactorily on various sections of the 1997–98 State Educational Assessment Program (SEAP) and the percentile change between those scores and 1996–97 school-year scores. As is evident, all building scores declined in math. All but one declined in reading (and in the case of the one building that increased, scores are still less than 60-percent satisfactory). Only three buildings improved writing scores, though all buildings continue to exceed 60-percent satisfactory. Only two buildings improved in science and, in both cases, fewer than half of students scored satisfactorily despite increased annual scores.

Building	Math 1997–1998	Percentage Change	Reading 1997–1998	Percentage Change
Elementary 1	84.6	-7.7	57.7	+25.8
Elementary 2	92.9	-8.6	60.5	-33.6
Elementary 3	82.9	-4.8	70.7	-21.9
Elementary 4	63.9	-20	38.5	-21.6
Elementary 5	75.4	-16	51.7	-23
Elementary 6	70.2	-10	53.2	-3.2
Elementary 7	50	-17	38.2	-9.9
Elementary 8	88.5	-11	68.5	-4.8

Building	Writing 1997–1998	Percentage Change	Science 1997–1998	Percentage Change
Elementary 1	78.9	+30.8	47.4	+9.4
Elementary 2	80	+20.8	32.3	-1.7
Elementary 3	63.9	-40	41.7	-2.9
Elementary 4	73.3	-14	49	+2.7
Elementary 5	66.7	-36	46.2	-16
Elementary 6	66.7	-43	36.7	-1
Elementary 7	62.5	-11	17.5	-20
Elementary 8	93.3	+7	57.4	-21

To mitigate the effects of rising poverty levels and improve SEAP scores, CPS must put the hardware and LAN/WAN network to use as the learning tools they are meant to be. All CPS school buildings score "low-tech" in the areas of content/software, professional development, and instructional integration and use. CPS's first technology plan (1997) held outcome objectives for students to become computer proficient, but it did not emphasize the use of technology in content areas as tools to enhance learning. Since that plan was written and filed, CPS has had several changes in administration, including a new technology director and a new assistant superintendent.

The assistant superintendent comes from direct experience in the schools, specifically as principal of a model elementary school, and understands the importance of integrating technology resources to improve academic outcomes. Both new administrators are in the process of revising the long-range technology plan and are committed to acquiring software, providing "just-in-time" training for teaching staff, and integrating the use of technology resources into all areas of instruction.

Note how the grant writer weaves in information about land use and makes it relevant to a grant proposing to address a need for technology resources among school children. Additionally, a STaR chart was used by the state to help schools measure the number of computers they had, the age of the computers, the uses of the technology, and the comfort level of teachers with the equipment. The numbers were then compiled into a final measure of low-tech, medium-tech, and high-tech to demonstrate need in the various categories.

Chapter 11

Writing Goals, Objectives, and Outcomes

No part of the proposal is more important than the goals, objectives, and outcomes, which are usually a part of—and integral to—the project description. The granting agency wants to know what their money will achieve, and they want to know what evidence you'll be supplying to ensure them they've made a difference.

What's the Distinction?

Goals are broad statements about what the program will accomplish or your mission(s) for the project. Outcomes are planned changes in the environment or people, and should be measurable. Objectives are the things that you'll plan to do in order to achieve outcomes, and must also be measurable. Other words you may encounter in describing goals, objectives, and outcomes include these:

Benchmarks: The places along the way that will mark your progress. Think of them as mini goals.

Activities: The specific steps you will take to achieve the objectives in the grant.

Indicators: The measures you will use to determine whether you have met the objectives or outcomes of the grant.

Inputs (resources): The items you'll need to carry out the objectives or activities (such as surveys, money, staff time, volunteer time, etc.).

Outputs: Direct products from program activities (number of service units, number of participants, products developed, curricula developed, etc.).

Timeline: A schedule for completion of objectives/activities with assigned responsibilities.

In the last decade, "measurable outcomes" have taken the place of "goals and objectives" in many RFPs; however, others still ask for all three.

Writing Goals: What Will You Accomplish?

Goals are the broad, overarching statements of purpose for your program. For instance, a lead-hazard program may state its goal as "reducing the risk of lead hazards to children in inner-city homes." A health clinic may state a goal as "ensuring translation services to all non–English-speaking clients."

Goals don't need to be measurable, and can be fairly broad since you must include support for each in the form of objectives, activities, outcomes, benchmarks, and/or indicators. Keep your goals realistic for the time frame of the grant and the money you are requesting. Remember that you must report on progress toward goals and outcomes at the end of, and sometimes during, the grant period, so you'll want to make sure that the goal statements describe objectives that your organization is relatively sure it can meet.

Writing Outcomes: What Will Change?

Outcomes are the basis for your evaluation plan. Ask yourself what will change as a result of your project and use the answers as outcomes. Then ask yourself how you will measure the change.

If you are implementing a project to make your local high school safer from school violence, you might plan on the following changes and measures that can be combined into an outcome statement:

What will change? Students will not bring weapons to school.

How will we know? Reduced number of students expelled for weapons; findings of random locker checks.

Outcome statement: As an outcome of the safer-schools program, results from four random locker checks will yield fewer weapons and at the end of year one; fewer students will have been expelled for weapons violations on school grounds.

What will change? Teachers will be able to identify behaviors indicative of propensity for school violence and take appropriate intervention measures.

How will we know? Number of teachers attending workshops provided by FBI school-violence specialist; number of teachers scoring high on workshop learning reviews; number of students referred to counseling for suspicious behaviors.

Outcome statement: As a result of workshops conducted by FBI school-violence specialists, teachers will be better equipped to identify behaviors that signal school violence and make appropriate system referrals for troubled students as indicated by an increased number of teacher referrals to counseling specialists and the reasons for referrals.

What will change? Fighting on school grounds will decrease.

How will we know? Fewer suspensions/expulsions for fighting; referrals for counseling; number of students participating in peer-dispute resolution sessions.

Outcome statement: Fighting on school grounds will decrease as indicated by comparative data on school disciplinary actions and by the number and results of student peer-dispute resolution sessions.

Some outcomes cannot be achieved during the grant period, even in a three-year funded project. When you report on your outcomes, you should be sure that you report progress toward the outcomes even when you cannot report having achieved the change(s) permanently.

Writing Objectives: What Will You Do?

Objectives are a running list of activities, projects, seminars, and other events or items you will produce, participate in, and/or use to achieve the goals and outcomes of a project. Objectives must be measurable.

Using the example of a safer-schools program, some objectives might include the following:

- At least 80 percent of staff members will attend at least one of three FBI-led seminars focusing on identifying indicators for school violence and possible actions teachers can take.
- At least thirty more students than last year will be referred for counseling services because of indicators for violence.
- At least fifty students will be trained to perform peer mediation. At least 400 students will participate in peer-mediation services in year one.
- Random locker checks will be performed four times during the school year.
- The school will rewrite its policies and procedures for dealing with violence on school grounds. New guidelines will be distributed to all students, signed, and returned to homeroom teachers. New guidelines will be mailed to 40,000 households in the school district that receive the district newsletter.

Note how the objectives include numbers so that the organization can quickly assess their progress any time during the project. Clear measures are also important to the grant writer if he or she is to write progress reports to the funder. Unlike outcomes, you must achieve as many of the objectives as possible and to the degree that you state. So while you're writing, be realistic.

Common Cents

Writing objectives is a balancing act. You have to promise to do enough to interest funders, yet not promise too much, setting your organization up for failure. The objectives must also link to the statement of need or problem and to the budget, so that the plan of work makes sense to the proposing organization and its potential funder.

It's nice to promise, for instance, that 100 percent of the teachers will attend a seminar, but it is more likely that at least 10 percent won't. If the teachers are not being reimbursed for their time, you may not be able to expect more than a 50-percent turnout. Discuss these eventualities candidly in your review of the writing to make sure that your client or employer can truly commit to the objectives.

Putting It All Together

Following is a program outline for Museums Are Fun for Everyone that includes goals, objectives, outcomes, and indicators. Note the differences in language used to respond to an RFP that called for a purpose statement, services, outcomes, and indicators.

Program Title
Museums Are Fun for Everyone

Program Purpose (Goal)

The Museum provides a series of workshops about its programs for mothers and two- to five-year olds from the Hills High School parenting program and Cabot Park neighborhood to increase visits by local families and to increase the museum comfort level of mothers who rarely or never visit the museum.

Program Services (Objectives)

1. Make outreach visits to Hills High School and Head Start parent meetings
2. Provide three Saturday workshops for target mothers and children
3. Provide three after-school workshops for target mothers and children

Intended Outcomes

Mothers from Cabot Park and Hills High will feel more comfortable bringing kids to the museum, and these families will visit the museum more often.

Indicators

(a) The number of participating mothers who report their comfort in bringing children to the museum increased to at least four on a five-point scale, and (b) the number of Cabot Park and Hills High visitors in Kids' Week 2009.

Data Source(s)

(a) Questionnaire and phone survey for all mothers who participate in a workshop and (b) random exit interviews of adults who visit the Museum with children during Kids' Week 2008, repeated in Kids' Week 2009.

Target for Change
(a) Participants' reported their comfort level goes up 75 percent or more from workshop one to six weeks after workshop three, and (b) visits by target families increase from less than 1 percent in Kids' Week 2008 to 10 percent in Kids' Week 2009. In the project described above, the goal is to increase the comfort level of mothers visiting the museum, with the longer-term goal of increasing museum visits by families. The project will ask mothers who participate in the workshops to rate their comfort level in the museum on a simple scale ("five equals very comfortable, one equals not at all comfortable") to show that mothers feel more comfortable in the museum after the workshops. During Kids' Weeks 2008 and 2009, it will compare information about where visitors live to see whether the workshop series increased visitors from the target neighborhoods.

Questionnaires and interviews provide the opportunity to ask other important planning questions and can be very short. There might be other explanations for a rise in local Kids' Week attendance, but if the museum did not make major changes in the program or publicity, it would be reasonable to think the workshops made a difference. Outcome-based evaluation has different goals from research or many visitor studies—it seeks to document the extent to which a program achieved its purposes.

Completing a Project Description
While the goals and objectives and outcomes are the most critical part of the project description, they are not the only components. You must also provide a narrative introduction and explanations,

often a timeline of activities, and a rationale for why you've chosen one method or project over another.

You may be asked to address several other issues or requirements within the section, including but not limited to the following:

- Stakeholder involvement in project design
- Partners to the project and their roles
- Research findings regarding the project
- Projected benefits to constituency
- Professional development activities related to the project
- Strategies
- Programmatic divisions and separate goals for each

The following sample is in response to a state Department of Education RFP that required a purpose statement and goals and objectives but that did not request outcomes. The available funds were targeted more toward capital expenses for technology equipment or infrastructure.

Insider Tip

Explain what the need is and link the response and the need statement through measurable objectives. Report local data using footnotes to support the use of research material, and describe how your community's needs are the same or worse than others in the nation.

In this sample response, the granting agent did not assume that an investment in technology would yield social or behavioral change, so it did not request outcome-based measurement.

Project Description

The purpose of the school district's technology project is to equip the district with a fiber-optic WAN/LAN and to deliver the professional development/training its staff requires to meet the following goals:

(a) Incorporate technology to teach to the state and district outcome standards;

(b) Report student achievement of standards to parents, district, and state officials;

(c) Improve teaching strategies and methodologies for all students; and

(d) Improve communication channels and outreach with parents and community members

All teachers will be required to attend at least fifteen hours of training in one or more of the following, depending on their proficiencies: CIMS, Word, Excel, PowerPoint, Internet, distance learning, using e-mail and listservs, website development, and multimedia. Teachers will also participate in multimedia training that will enable them to incorporate voice/video/data opportunities into their classrooms.

Four of the elementary buildings, for instance, have environmental projects dealing with plant life, water resources, air quality, and wetlands. Fiber-optic lines would provide video capabilities to enable the teachers to share their school-ground environmental laboratories across the district. Teachers could also use the voice-video-data transfers to address shared concerns, become members of interdistrict learning groups, or communicate with the administrative office or parents of their students.

Classes for teachers on distance learning and maximizing their use of the fiber-optic WAN/LAN will be offered during the school year on release time or on an alternate schedule as proposed by staff.

Within one year, teachers will submit information about curriculum, homework, and standards for addition to the district website. Teachers will be encouraged and supported to develop their own websites to enhance communication with students, parents, and community members. In addition, teachers will develop e-mail connections between themselves and parents/ students so that parents might contact teachers regarding specific questions about their children and students can submit homework or questions electronically.

Students without home computers will be encouraged to access websites from the multimedia computer labs in the upper-grade buildings and from the media-room computer in elementary schools. All students, beginning in third grade, will participate in at least one e-mail correspondence with their teacher(s).

Goals and Activities

Goals and activities/objectives are summarized here:

1. Incorporate technology to teach to the state and district outcome standards; to report student achievement of standards to parents, district, and state officials; and to improve teaching strategies and methodologies for all district students.

    Objective 1.1: By December, 2002, install fiber-optic WAN-LAN to intra- and interconnect all school buildings.

    Objective 1.2: By August, 2003, connect Student-Report System software for tracking student achievement of standards, attendance, course outlines, and syllabi. Select software that can look for trends among standards and desegregate student achievement by standard.

    Objective 1.3: By July, 2003, connect all computers to the district's intranet and to the Internet.

Objective 1.4: By June, 2004, provide professional development courses in distance learning and use of VVD lines to share classroom activities.

2. Improve communication channels and outreach with parents and community members.

Objective 2.1: By December, 2003, establish a district-wide e-mail system.

Objective 2.2: By December, 2003, require teachers to submit information for inclusion on district website.

Objective 2.3: By June, 2004, establish listservs to facilitate communication between teachers and parents.

Tips that you can learn from this sample include the following:

- Whenever possible, provide concrete examples of program activities or strategies. It makes the project come alive for the reader and assures them that you really plan to move from theory to action.
- When neither the grant money nor the organization can ensure equal access to programs or equipment by all the target population, you must provide a solution. In this case, kids without home computers can use the media center at the school in the evening.
- It's not enough to apply for grants to purchase computers because your school needs them. Explain what you'll use them for and how they will improve educational outcomes for all students.

Chapter 12

Writing Action Plans and Timelines

Most RFPs request a fully detailed plan of action—a step-by-step explanation of what the grantee organization will do and when. An action plan is the detailed map to achieving your goal. In this chapter, you'll learn various ways of developing a detailed plan of action that answers the requirements of the RFP.

What Are Action Steps?

In the same way that objectives are the steps toward achieving a goal, action steps are the next level of detail, the steps your organization will take to achieve the objective. For each objective you've listed, ask yourself how you will achieve that objective. For instance, following is the list of hypothetical objectives from Chapter 11.

- At least thirty more students will be referred for counseling services because of indicators for violence than were last year.
- At least fifty students will be trained to perform peer mediation. At least 400 students will participate in peer-mediation services in year one.
- Random locker checks will be performed four times during the school year.
- The school will rewrite its policies and procedures for dealing with violence on school grounds.
- New guidelines will be distributed to all students, signed, and returned to homeroom teachers.
- New guidelines will be mailed to 40,000 households in the school district that receive the district newsletter.

The next step is to develop a plan to describe how you will achieve the objectives. Think about what it will take to do that. What will it take for a school to perform four random locker checks during the school year? At minimum, they will have to do the following: (a) identify a means for random selection of lockers; (b) plan a schedule to ensure that they perform the inspections four times within the nine-month school year; (c) identify what inspectors should look for during the inspections; (d) communicate the plan and goal to inspectors; and (e) develop a plan for reporting findings.

To fulfill the spirit of the objective, they also must have a plan ready for what they will do if they find drugs, guns, knives, or other contraband in the lockers. This step, however, would be better if made a part of the fourth objective to rewrite the school's policies and procedures for dealing with violence on school grounds.

Who's Responsible?

An integral part of an action plan is assignment of responsibility, and by definition, accountability. In the example of random locker checks, assignment would likely go to the high school principal. It would be up to the principal to then assign inspectors, help identify the means of random selection, and ensure that the objective is met with no fewer than four locker inspections during the year.

Insider Tip

Remember that you are adding additional responsibilities to someone's job by assigning action steps. Try to have high-level administrators at your organization check with people before redefining or expanding their responsibilities. Grant money won't be used to increase pay for increased work.

Responsibility for training teachers to fulfill the first objective would fall to the district administrators. After training, it would fall to the teachers, and then, ultimately, when you address accountability for achieving the objective, to the principal directly in charge of the teachers.

The organization implementing a funded project must assign responsibility for each objective or each step in the action plan, whether requested by the RFP or not. You can do that during the writing process by developing a grid or narrative that assigns responsibility. You can always change those reporting channels later if you need to. For instance, if between application and funding, the principal retires, the district might want to reassign responsibility to the vice principal, because she has been in the school and is familiar with personnel and existing procedures.

The granting agent rarely, if ever, cares exactly who is responsible for achieving an objective, so long as the person is judged competent by position, education, or reputation. But they will care very much if the objective goes unfilled. Ultimately, if the funded organization fails to achieve its objectives, someone will be held accountable!

How Long It Takes to Achieve Goals

Nearly everything takes longer than you think it will. It's true about writing the grant narrative, and it's especially true about implementing a project. Grant awards are most often for one year or three years. If you have a one-year grant, you have to be very realistic in writing your plans about what can be accomplished in one year. With three-year grants you have more latitude in planning your timeline and meeting your goals.

One-Year Projects

With a one-year project, you must make sure that your agency can accomplish what it sets out to do and that it can achieve or make progress toward the outcomes in one year or less. One-year action plans must be very detailed. Think of the year as being the first step in a long process of change—it will take longer than the grant period to reach your desired outcomes. Therefore, action plans should list just those steps your organization can make in one year, not all the effort that will take place later to achieve the outcome.

Insider Tip

Assign every step, from developing a job description for a new position to hiring that person; from sending out product bid requests to purchasing them. This is a good way to give your organization time to plan and put things into place before you launch the project.

One way to handle this task is by structuring the timeline for a year-long funded project by each month of the year, beginning in the month that the organization is likely to receive the grant funding.

Multiyear Projects

If you are applying for a multiyear grant (usually three years), you must submit a three-year action plan. In three years you can come closer to achieving an outcome for change, so you can use many of your objectives and outcomes as the framework for a three-year action plan.

You don't have to be exact in your timeline. Provide a month-by-month breakdown for year one, and a much more generic timeline for years two and three, incorporating only recurring activities and next steps in the process that began in year one. At the end of the first year, write out a detailed action plan for year two. This will help you accomplish your stated goals in the time allotted.

Detailed Action Plans

If you are asked to write a detailed action plan, it's implied (if not stated) that the grantor wants a timeline of activities. It's sometimes easier to develop a plan of action by asking yourself what needs to be done first, second, third, and so on, so your thought process becomes the structure of the plan. The third sample at the end of this chapter provides a simple illustration of a timeline-centered plan of action.

Illustrating Goals

As stated earlier in this chapter, sometimes the questions about action plans, persons responsible, and the time frame of activities are asked as separate questions. More often, the RFP requests "a detailed plan of action that includes objectives, measures, persons responsible, action steps, and a time frame for accomplishments."

Using Grids

In these cases, a grid is the most efficient way of communicating all the required information in a short amount of space. Cells or tables available in most word-processing computer programs make such illustrations simple. Remember, however, that you will sometimes have six or more columns if you separate each topic.

Common Cents

Print grids horizontally. Extensively detailed action plans are best constructed on landscape-oriented pages. You may even want to write the entire grant narrative on landscape-oriented pages so readers don't have to turn pages.

Using Diagrams

Process-oriented projects often require a diagram to illustrate the steps in planning. Continuous improvement, for instance, is a cyclical rather than a linear process. Grids don't work to illustrate concepts like the process of planning, implementing, checking, and revising, which can be ongoing and may start anywhere in the process. Instead, illustrate these concepts with simple diagrams like the one below.

Using Typeface and Gray-Scale Techniques

Most RFPs will specify that they do not want color graphs or charts. But when illustrating levels of information, you can use various fonts, typefaces, simple black-and-white graphs, gray-scale shading, and tables. Just be sure that your illustrations photocopy well. Copy that's lost in an improperly shaded box, for instance, counters your attempts to be clear and concise in your action plan.

Sample Action Plans

The first sample action plan was developed for a health-care clinic. Organized by life-cycle stages (perinatal, pediatric, adolescent, adult, and geriatric), it begins with a problem statement. Each problem then has a set of goals, objectives, action steps, and evaluation measures.

Note that timelines and the person responsible for each step are incorporated into the chart. For instance, each objective begins with "By this month" (in correlation with the timeline), and each evaluation statement tells who is responsible for evaluating progress toward the objective. Timelines and responsibility assignments also may be called out separately in action plans.

These three different ways of presenting a timeline demonstrate the flexibility you'll have for presenting the requested information clearly and concisely, in a form that does not eat up excessive amounts of your page limits.

Following is an action plan organized under a problem statement, showing a set of goals and objectives for the named problem.

LIFE-CYCLE-STAGE ORGANIZATION

Problem/Need Statement: The population of this state ranks highest in the United States in incidence of chronic disease illness. "Healthy County 2010" targets reducing preventable chronic disease incidence and mortality, focusing on cancer (173.8 per 100,000), cardiovascular disease and stroke (231.6 per

100,000), and diabetes (approximately 26,570 individuals). The poverty and cultures of the clinic's geriatric patients contribute to their high risk of developing one or more chronic illnesses. The clinic sees many patients for episodic care only and has developed objectives to increase prevention services to these patients.

Goal (funding): To increase education about prevention and treatment for clinic's geriatric patients, thereby working to reduce incidence and mortality due to chronic diseases. (CHC funding)

Objectives

J1: By December, 2008, 70 percent of all patients who visit will have had an annual risk assessment completed during an episodic visit in a calendar year. Risk assessments will include, as applicable: offers for health-maintenance exam; pap test; immunizations and boosters; cancer screening; anemia testing; cardiovascular screening; prostate screening; mammograms; diabetes screening; and screening for depression, ADL, smoking/ alcohol/ substance abuse, oral nutrition, and morbid obesity.

J2: By December, 2008, provide medication review for 8 percent of geriatric patients at risk of drug interactions.

Action Steps

J1.a. Revise risk-assessment forms for geriatric life cycles (change colors each year to indicate calendar year in which each risk assessment was completed).

J1.b. Providers document risk assessments performed.

J1.c. Providers document risk-management plans in place, if indicated.

J2.a. Add appropriate questions to patient-progress note forms; e.g., "Has patient seen other providers since last visit?" "What medicines has patient been prescribed by other providers?" "What over-the-counter medications is patient taking?" Document responses.

J2.b. Audit progress notes to ensure that providers ask questions.

Evaluation and Data
J1. Quarterly audits of ten randomly selected geriatric patient charts performed by coordinator. Results reported to medical director.

J2. Revised patient progress notes: clinical coordinator to audit quarterly ten randomly selected geriatric patient charts. Results reported to medical director.

Comments
See appendix for same risk-assessment sheets, which will be revised.

Horizontal Landscape
The second example is from a community problem-solving organization. This horizontal (landscape) timeline is a good way to graph activities that are scheduled to take place over a period of months, a year, or more. You'll see activities for five months in this sample.

	Month 1	Month 2	Month 3	Month 4	Month 5
Activity A	Observe funder staff-systems thinking workshop	Participate in leadership planning for final visioning retreat	Synthesize learning from previous activities	Identify and attend at least one community meeting	Continue community engagement; tri-weekly design-team meetings
	Hold ABC focus groups		Identify and attend at least one community meeting		Identify and attend at least one community meeting
Activity B	Triweekly meetings of design team for community engagement process		Hold first systems thinking workshop for twenty-four diverse leaders as nominated/selected from advisory committee and leadership	Synthesize learning from first-systems thinking workshop	Synthesize learning from community meetings
	Identify and attend at least one community meeting				
Associated costs		$3,000 (facilitators, food for activity B)	$12,000 (facilitator materials, food, lodging, logistics, for activity B)	$5,000 (facility, facilitators, publicity, and materials for activity A, which continues for several months)	

Timeline Example

The last sample is a simple timeline of a year's activities for each of the first twelve months. Begin a timeline with the month in which funding is likely to be approved. Whether as dots on a chart or in narrative form, be sure to identify recurring activities throughout the project. Also, continuous improvement is, by definition, recurring and continuous. Be sure to illustrate evaluation steps that lend themselves to constant review and program revision.

June: Announce to local media memberships of partner organizations and citizens, the grant award, and launch of the commission. Finalize job description and seek applicants for project coordinator.

July: Interview and select project coordinator.

Monthly: Convene meetings of commission; select and schedule speakers and/or expert consultants for gathering information and sharing lessons learned.

August–January: Gather data from Information Infrastructure providers, businesses, and others needed to identify current infrastructure.

January: Map current public-access sites and disseminate to sites frequented by those who are believed to lack access to computer equipment. (Note: This activity is funded by the Community Foundation.) Hold "town meeting" to encourage input by commission nonmembers on issues regarding technology infrastructure and digital divide.

January–April: With professional facilitator and available data, develop vision, key findings, and recommendations for the Information Infrastructure.

April: Perform SWOT on data, findings, and draft recommendations; identify gaps between preferred infrastructure and existing infrastructure.

May: Begin mapping process for inclusion in commission report. Report evaluation of the planning process and grant expenditures.

Balancing Ambition with Realism

Often, once an organization has been granted funding, its members suddenly feel overwhelmed looking at the action plan and think, "How are we going to get all this done in a year?" This is a common struggle. Most nonprofits just don't have the capacity to be ready to launch a new program the minute they are awarded the funding. Often, the project implementation schedule is two or three months, sometimes more, behind the schedule (timeline) that was included in the proposal.

The grant writer must strike a balance between setting forth an action plan and schedule that are sufficiently ambitious to get the grant and setting a schedule that is realistic. And it's not only because the organization will struggle to get started—many grants are turned down because the action plan is unrealistic.

Insider Tip

Set aside the first month or two of your action plan for tasks your organization can accomplish quickly or somewhat easily while you prepare to implement the newly funded project. For instance, include time to post a new job opening and interview candidates, or announce the grant award to the media.

Be thorough and detailed. Promise enough work on behalf of your client or employer to accomplish the stated goals, but not so much that even the grant readers shake their heads in disbelief.

Also be sure to write a paragraph about the capacity of the organization. Will it need additional staff to lead or carry out the project? Schedule at least thirty days early in the action plan for finding those people.

Chapter 13

Designing an Evaluation Plan

Evaluators have their own language, and you need to learn to use this language when writing grant-program evaluations, not only because the evaluation is a critical part of the grant proposal, but because using the language of evaluators adds authority to your grant writing.

Speak Their Language

This list includes some of the most common terminology:

Qualitative: Means of measuring objectives with "soft" data, including opinion surveys, anecdotal stories from participants and staff, etc. Remember the root word "quality" to determine the difference between qualitative and quantitative.

Quantitative: Means of measuring objectives with "hard" data (that is, numbers). Remember the root word "quantity" to determine the difference between quantitative and qualitative.

Operationalize: Act of forming measurable outcomes from aims and goals of the grant program.

Longitudinal study: Study of change over a specified time period.

Anecdotal evidence: Stories from participants or staff. A part of a qualitative (soft data) measure.

Indicators: Selection of measures that will determine success.

Learning history: Particular type of evaluation, useful for projects that are highly process-oriented and do not lend themselves to quantitative evaluation. Formed from written documents such as meeting minutes and interviews of participants. This type of evaluation is mostly qualitative.

Assessment: Measurement tool.

Continuous improvement: Use of indicators and evaluation to determine ways the project can improve its services.

Benchmarks: Data on the current status of the problem that the evaluator can use to measure subsequent changes.

You don't have to be a professional evaluator to write an evaluation, but you do need to speak the language.

Types of Evaluations

There are internal, external, and national evaluations. Internal evaluations are those performed by project personnel as a part of the project. Typically, the organization hires an outside consultant to perform an external evaluation.

National evaluations are cross-organizational, cross-project evaluations performed by the granting agency to determine the effectiveness of a particular type of project in its various geographic locations. These types of evaluations are called "cluster evaluations."

Insider Tip

National evaluations are strong learning tools for all participants. They share results of all their evaluations as well as plans, remedial efforts to fix what doesn't work, and success stories. The comparisons between similar projects implemented with different populations and in different locations are interesting and often provide information that you can use in your next community problem-solving effort.

Mandatory Evaluations

Sometimes an RFP will mandate an external evaluation or both an external and a national evaluation project. If an external evaluator has to be called in, the granting agency will mandate a budget line item and most often will cover the cost. It's often a percentage of the overall grant request. If your agency participates in a national evaluation project, there are no extra charges.

External Evaluations

When an external evaluation is commissioned, it is likely to be performed by a nearby or state university/college department, by the local United Way, or by a national organization under which your organization operates (such as a media-technology support organization, a health-studies group, etc.). When the type of evaluation is not predetermined, you and your organization can choose the most appropriate means of evaluating the project, as well as the person who will perform it.

Evaluating Small Projects

Generally, the smaller the grant request the less stringent the grantor is about the form of the evaluation. Small grants may be evaluated by something as simple as a survey developed by project staff that asks participants about their impressions of a new building façade or what they learned at a seminar or whatever else was funded.

Insider Tip

Sometimes, you can write a grant proposal requesting money just for evaluation. If your project is up and running, you might ask the local United Way or community foundation to fund a learning history or a cost-effectiveness study. If you think your project might have potential for replication of results in other communities, you might ask an independent foundation to fund an evaluation to determine all the factors that contributed to your success.

Asking the Right Questions

The best way to begin an evaluation plan is to ask yourself what you and the grantor hope to achieve or learn, then develop a process to identify and measure your success.

The following list of questions was developed for a long-term community-improvement project involving public transportation. The agency recognized that it would take a number of years to see any meaningful changes taking place in the use of public transportation and the habits of people in the community. Nevertheless, the agency wanted to measure any small steps taken in that direction. To do it, the agency decided to conduct an annual evaluation.

- Have we developed a shared vision statement for improving transportation that is accepted by the entire community? Is the statement applicable to all social, environmental, and economic issues?
- What has been our work with existing community initiatives? Has there been progress in merging like initiatives, particularly those that are cross-cluster or cross-sector? Is participation in these initiatives increasing, and does participation reflect the community's diversity?
- Are participants in events and meetings surrounding the project and its action teams diverse in age, ethnicity, income, gender, residence, and opinion?
- Are problem-solving models and strategies readily available? Are they being requested? Used?
- Have we collected and shared data? To what degree? What is missing?
- What are the agreed-on measures of success? Are benchmarks available for all areas of agreement?
- With what communities have we communicated to share information and lessons? What new connections among individuals,

organizations, and/or sectors have grown from the project and its transportation action team?

Weigh both the grantor and grantee goals. Be sure to ask both questions: What does your organization hope to learn? What does the granting agent hope to learn? Hopefully, they are the same. If not, blend the questions together to form the basis for your evaluation plan.

Determining Results

Once the questions are listed, ask yourself how you can find the answers. For instance, in the questions posed above, how will the organization find out if its action teams are diverse? Clearly, the organization must survey participants to determine their opinions, gender, age, ethnicity, income, and neighborhood.

If the organization asks about gender, it will become apparent after just a few meetings if it lacks women. Then it can target that group to ensure (the operative word signaling success of the evaluation criteria) that the action teams become a good cross-section of participants.

In the first evaluation sample at the end of this chapter, one of the things the organization wants to learn is the long-term effect of a ninth-grade adventure-camp experience. The evaluator, therefore, might be asked to develop a series of surveys and other evaluative tools to test the effects. One could take place at the end of the camping experience, a second at the end of ninth grade, and the others could be scheduled annually thereafter. This might be the best way to determine whether the learning at the adventure camp has changed the lives of its participants, either for better or worse, and whether any short-term changes were sustained over time.

An evaluation of a hypothesis (for instance, that ninth graders will have a life-altering experience at an adventure camp) need not be proven true in order to have a successful evaluation. The evaluation is a success even if the hypothesis turns out to be false.

Linking Evaluation to Goals and Objectives

If you've written strong goals and objectives, half the work of writing the evaluation section is complete. Return to your project plan. Pull out every objective or outcome, and repeat it in this section. Use the indicators you developed for the objectives/outcomes, if any, or establish indicators in the evaluation section as the measures of effectiveness for each of your objectives.

The strongest grant proposals make the link between the project goals and objectives and the evaluation plan. If your goal is to increase use of the public transportation system and you have objectives regarding marketing, additional stops for buses, new times for bus routes, and similar efforts, you can develop an evaluation plan that addresses the overall success toward reaching your goal. In this case, you would measure ridership both before (baseline) and after implementation of the objectives. Then you can determine whether the steps the transit authority took had the desired effect on the goal (that is, increasing use of the public transportation system).

Sample Evaluation Plans

The following sample was written to address an RFP mandate for a local (external) evaluator to be hired by the project. The RFP also stipulated that the evaluation would be coordinated with a national evaluation process for all similar projects in the United States that were designed and funded by the federal grantor.

This grant proposal lists the numerous components of a program that addresses the entire life cycle (infants to seniors) and, therefore, requires extensive evaluation to address each of the components.

The school district and its local partners to the project agree to participate in a national evaluation of the Safe Schools–Healthy Students Initiative, which will collect data on student-risk indicators and outcomes of the programs implemented across sites on an annual basis. Further, the local evaluator will:

- Help district strategically plan activities that will achieve the program goals and objectives
- Respond to the direction of the national evaluator to ensure the collection of high-quality core data
- Design and implement a process evaluation of the local program with assistance from the national evaluator to show results achieved as appropriate
- Provide district with data that can be used to make adjustments in service delivery and improve the overall program
- Design and conduct an outcome evaluation to determine whether an intervention is producing its intended effects

Specifically, the local evaluator, Dr. T. of State University's School of Public Administration and director of the Office of Community Research, will assist the partnership in all forms of interim, annual, and final evaluations. She will teach staff how to gather and log appropriate data to track the progress of the district's Safe Schools–Healthy Students Initiative and all students.

Academic and other appropriate data on all students will be gathered continuously by district staff as advised by the local evaluator and reviewed quarterly in reports to the project partners to ensure immediate responses to weaknesses in the plan.

The Search Institute survey of assets was given to district seventh, ninth, and eleventh graders in 2004 and in 2006 and is scheduled to be given again in 2008. In this way, the district is able to gather comparative data on cohorts of young people (i.e., the ninth graders tested in 2006 were mostly the same seventh graders tested in 2004). The year 2008 asset-survey responses will provide a baseline measure of assets early in the proposed process of involving the entire community in building assets. A fourth survey (second during the grant period) in 2008 will measure the effect of the community process on the youth.

Healthy Communities–Healthy Youth has compiled the following list of fifteen characteristics of asset-building communities. The local evaluator will operationalize these characteristics to establish benchmark measures for the city community in the first year of the grant. By the end of the three-year process, the district and its partners will have demonstrated progressive development in each of the characteristics listed:

1. All residents take personal responsibility for building assets in children and adolescents.
2. The community thinks and acts intergenerationally.
3. The community builds a consensus on values and boundaries that it seeks to articulate and model.
4. All children and teenagers frequently engage in service to others.
5. Families are supported, educated, and equipped to elevate asset building to top priority.
6. All children and teenagers receive frequent expressions of support in both informal settings and in places where youth gather.
7. Neighborhoods are places of caring, support, and safety.
8. Schools—both elementary and secondary—mobilize to promote caring, clear boundaries and sustained relationships with adults.
9. Businesses establish family-friendly policies and embrace asset-building principles for young employees.
10. Virtually all youth ten to eighteen years old are involved in one or more club, team, or other youth-serving organizations that see building assets as central to their mission.
11. The media (print, radio, television) repeatedly communicate the community's vision, support local mobilization efforts, and

provide forums for sharing innovative actions taken by individuals and organizations.

12. All professionals and volunteers who work with youth receive training in asset building.

13. Youth have opportunities to serve, lead, and make decisions.

14. Religious institutions mobilize their resources to build assets both within their own programs and in the community.

15. The community-wide commitment to asset building is long term and sustained.

Within the first six months of the grant period, the local evaluator will design a plan for evaluating all components of the initiative including, but not necessarily limited to:

- A longitudinal study of the effect of ninth-grade retreat camp on the students' high school careers and number of assets

- A sample population study of at least thirty toddlers from high-risk families and the effect of parent training/counseling and educational intervention on development and/or kindergarten readiness

- A comparison of all sociological and academic data gathered in each of the three years of the grant project indicating reductions in such things as truancy/expulsion, dropping out, disputes in schools, teen depression, teen pregnancy, experimentation with alcohol/drugs, juvenile crime, reports of abuse/neglect, and increases in state-assessment test scores and academic performance against district outcome standards

- A sample study of at least ten high-risk teens identified as potentially violent and the effect of intervention services on behavior and attitude

- A comparative study on reported feelings of "safety" among students in each of the building levels: elementary, middle, freshman, and high school

Narrative Evaluation Plan

Here's another sample evaluation plan. This one employs what is known as a "log frame" model. A log frame, or logic model, uses the goals and objectives of the organization's work plan as the basis for continuous evaluation and improvement. You can learn more about logic-model evaluation from your local United Way.

Defining and Measuring Success: This project will employ a Log Frame Model (also known as Logic Model) and Participatory Evaluation Process to evaluate effectiveness against a set of indicators. The methodology employs an independent evaluator working with program participants, ensures that evaluation is continuous, and involves program participants (e.g., family members, staff, and collaboration partners).

The independent evaluator will work with an evaluation team composed of neighborhood captains, family members from affected households, program staff, and members of the collaboration throughout the process. He or she will create the Log Frame Model and meet twice monthly with the evaluation team to track progress on the Logic Model and to measure effectiveness against indicators the team will establish to determine progress toward and effectiveness of the planned outcomes, goals and objectives, and activities of the project plan.

Evaluation Dissemination and Project Replication: Quarterly, the evaluator will provide a written report to the collaboration steering committee. The evaluator will provide an annual compilation report that will be made available to the collaboration steering committee and project funders. It will be the responsibility of the collaboration steering committee, working with the staff, to adjust the Logic Model in response to the findings of the evaluation team in order to maximize effectiveness of the project.

Once finalized and launched, the project model will be sent to the national foundation with a request for any information the foundation may have on other models for reducing lead hazard in the nation and for review as a replicable model for other communities.

Constituency Involvement in Evaluation: The Logic Model of evaluation includes constituents of the program in all aspects of evaluation.

Chapter 14

Developing a Budget and Budget Narrative

As you're developing the program, you'll also need to develop the budget needed to support the objectives. Perhaps there is an accountant within the organization who can work with you, but more often you will be responsible for writing the budget and budget narrative yourself.

How Much Can You Request?

Federal requests for proposals always list the total amount of money the department expects to have available for that project and a ceiling amount that they will grant to each successful project. Foundations, on the other hand, give a range of grant sizes and a typical grant. So they might write in the guidelines or catalog: "Range: $500 to $5,000. Typical grant size: $1,000."

When wealthy individuals who don't have a foundation give financial gifts, it's based on this formula, in this order:

1. Who asks
2. How they ask
3. What they ask for

While foundations do not operate based on "who asks," sometimes decisions that don't necessarily make sense to outsiders are made for reasons known only to those on the inside.

When to Ask for More

Follow your best intuition and best information about previous giving when you want to solicit a local foundation. Or simply ask the program officer directly if he can recommend a way to increase your request.

One grant writer we know once called a program officer and asked if they'd consider 5 percent of a capital campaign. The program officer told her that if this was for an organization the foundation would generally support, they might consider 10 percent, and said the grant writer could apply for 10 percent with the understanding that she might get less.

Common Cents
Never ask for cents in a grant proposal, such as $272,241.22. And never use cents in your budget presentation—stick with whole dollar amounts. Also, try to round up or down to the nearest $5 or $10 for your budget line items.

When Less Is Better
On federal or state grants, never exceed the highest amount on the range of grant funds. In fact, it's wiser to ask for less. It's also wise to ask for an unusual amount, such as $272,241 if the published cap is $300,000. An unrounded number infers that you are asking only for the funding absolutely necessary to implement the project. It also tells them that you have gone into great detail in your search for pricing on budget line items.

Match Requirements
Match requirements are those monies required to "leverage" or qualify for a grant. That means that the applicant must, through its operations budget or other donations—such as in-kind donations of time, space, products, and/or staffing—offer a certain amount of funds in order to qualify for the grant. Most often, match is required up front by federal and state granting agencies. It can also be stipulated in the grant agreement established by foundations after you have received notice of a successful application.

Match Tied to Sustainability Plans

Match is also linked to sustainability plans. For instance, the RFP may state that in year one, the applicant must provide a 25-percent match ($25 for every $100 requested); in year two, a 50-percent match; and in year three, a 75-percent match.

Insider Tip

One good way to provide part of a cash match, particularly if you are asking for staff salaries in the grant, is to have a willing applicant donate the new staff person's benefits package as a cash match. (Benefits are usually calculated at 25 to 30 percent of the salary.)

These requirements are meant to encourage the applicant to begin planning immediately to incorporate the project into its annual budget by year four, when the grant expires. It also has the result of discouraging applications by organizations that are more interested in pursuing grant money than in implementing and sustaining a necessary service.

Read the fine print in the RFP regarding matching requirements. Is it a combination of allowable expenses or must it be a cash match?

Federal Financial-Match Example

An RFP from the U.S. Department of Education says applicants receiving grant funds must maintain and document local resources at the following ratio:

Year one: at least 10 percent of total project cost

Year two: at least 20 percent of total project cost

Year three: at least 30 percent of total project cost

Year four: at least 40 percent of total project cost

Years five through eight: at least 50 percent of total project cost

Years nine through twelve: at least 65 percent of total project cost

The eligible applicant's share may be obtained from any source, including funds made available for programs under Title I, and may be provided in cash or as in-kind goods and services. All match items must be designated for the purposes of this project and must not be used to provide match to any other project.

To determine match, the requested amount is divided by the percentage that is the federal share of the project. Thus, a first-year project requesting $125,000 in federal funds will need to match with at least $13,888 ($125,000 divided by .90 = $138,888). To maintain that level of funding in the second year, the match would need to be increased to $31,250 ($125,000 divided by .80 = $156,250).

In-Kind Support

In-kind support refers to those things that the organization and its partners, if any, are offering in addition to or in lieu of money. In-kind support includes such contributions as the following:

Staff time: This is necessary when staff participate in such things as collaborative planning with others and are not paid additional wages for that participation.

Space and utilities: If an organization is providing office space for a staff person, rent, and utilities for the space usually qualifies as an in-kind donation. This amount is usually available from the organization's accountant, who has computed the cost of square footage and operational overhead (electricity, gas, etc.) to determine the value of a space donation. Telephone expenses may also be included in the cost per square foot.

Volunteer hours: Volunteer hours can be computed based on the average amount you would pay for comparable services in your community times the number of hours you can guarantee will be allocated to this project.

Products: Existing products (such as desks and computer equipment) that merely have to be moved to an office for a new staff person count as in-kind donations. New-product donations (for instance, software donated to a nonprofit organization) can be added as "cash match" if you document the value of the donation. Purchasing new equipment such as computers, furnishings, or telephones to support a staff position may be requested of grant funds or purchased by the applicant and offered as match.

Multiyear Requests

The RFP will define whether the program and the request must cover one or more years. Most foundations leave it open to the grant seeker whether to apply for one or more years of funding, but generally do not make grants longer than three years. Multiyear projects have their pluses and minuses. First, on the plus side, a project that is funded for three years is pretty much assured of continuation funding at the level it really needs to prove itself.

The only instance in which the grantor will take away second and third year funds is if the grantee does not comply with the grant agreement. Before that happens, however, the grantee is likely to receive a warning and a set of goals it must achieve prior to being given year-two funding.

The negative side of multiyear requests is that it's difficult to plan anything three years in advance, whether for programming or budget. Granting agencies understand this, however, and provide some latitude in the level of detail you must provide for second- and third-year budgets and details of the project.

In planning a three-year budget, you will have to accomplish two competing objectives. You must decrease grant funds over each of the years, and at the same time, increase costs (such as salaries) that are likely to go up each year. Here is a sample multiyear budget that one grant writer prepared for one of her clients:

Expense	Year 1	Year 2	Year 3
Personnel	114,500	214,550	226,950
Operating	45,550	35,450	38,050
TOTAL	160,050	250,000	265,000
Grant funding	80,000	120,000	80,000
Match funding	80,000	130,000	185,000

In this grant writer's multiyear-budget example, the organization planned to receive grants totaling $80,000 in year one to leverage (qualify for) a state money match of $80,000. In year two, it had to raise $120,000, and in year three, $80,000. Granting agencies are inclined to view grants that leverage other donations favorably.

Taking Care of Partners

If you are required to have partners in order to qualify for a grant program, then you must make sure that the partners are compensated for the services they provide under the project.

The federal Safe Schools–Healthy Students program grant, for instance, requires partnership among school districts, mental-health services, and police. It also requires the school district to be the primary applicant and fiduciary (the "accountant") on the grant.

The successful school-district applicant, therefore, must purchase the services of police and mental-health organizations in order to fulfill the requirements of the funded program. And while you are writing the grant proposal, costs for these services must be determined and calculated as part of the budget.

Other purchased services, such as evaluation, are also calculated before you submit the proposal, so it's best to ask for estimates when you meet with all the project partners to design the program.

Planning for Sustainability

Before seeking a grant, those involved must discuss the financial and programmatic needs that the project will have at the end of the grant period. Often, you can counsel them to request one-time purchases (such as computers, furnishings, supplies, or cars) from a grant and put less of the award toward ongoing costs such as staff salaries and benefits. They'll eventually have to pay staff salaries out of the organization's budget anyway, unless the project is abandoned. And, if the project is likely to be abandoned after the grant runs out, how valuable was it in addressing a need or problem? Should it have been proposed in the first place?

Sustaining programs after the grant period is the latest big issue with foundations and government funders. They have grown weary of helping to establish programs only to see them disappear for want of funds, energy, or commitment after their grant money is used. They are now requiring that every grant proposal include a discussion about sustaining the project after grant funds are expended. Here are some possible methods of sustaining programs:

- Charge a copay or small fee for services to offset costs.
- Charge as many one-time costs as possible to the grant (e.g., equipment, training, etc.) and begin to incorporate ongoing costs (e.g., space, staff, etc.) into the nonprofit's annual budget.
- Find an ongoing resource, such as a Community Mental Health Fund or per-pupil allocation from the state that indicates a willingness or interest in funding the project after it has proved itself.
- Plan an annual fundraising event from which proceeds will support the project.

- Address the problem or need permanently within the time frame of the grant so there are no ongoing costs.

Writing the Budget Narrative

Whether you actually write the budget yourself or you receive one from your executive director or accountant, you do have to write the budget narrative. The narrative is your chance to explain how you developed this budget. Your narrative should include the following details:

Calculations: If the project requires two full-time-equivalent (FTE) counselors, each working forty hours per week at $40,000 per year, you budget $80,000 per year. Over three years they will cost $240,000. (If you need two half-time staff per year, you should request one FTE.)

Other sources of funding, if any, and their use.

Distribution of funding for the line item: "Part from matching funds, part from the grant request."

Justification: "$40,000 annual is the average salary of a certified counselor in this area."

Estimated or actual cost: "The cost of software packages is $222 each if purchased through the state plan for mass purchases. ABC, therefore, requests twenty packages at an actual cost of $4,440." Or you can say, "Software packages are estimated at $225 each times twenty for a request of $4,500."

Remember to include only the costs relating to the particular program and not ongoing administration costs that are not part of the grant proposal, unless you are applying for a general operating grant or attributing the cost to the "indirect" line item. You might even explain what will become of equipment after the project is over.

A budget includes both expenses and revenue; don't neglect to address the revenue side of the budget. Where will all the necessary funding come from?

Citing Other Sources of Funding

Whether you are or are not required to provide in-kind or matching funds, you must indicate where you will be receiving all the funding necessary to complete the project. Take a look at the example at the end of this chapter—it is a budget for launching a project that later received federal funding.

Another example is in the foundation grant proposal in Appendix D. The grant applicant stated the source of all matching donations in the budget narrative, including the $80,000 it received from a previously successful grant cited in the sample budget at the end of this chapter. If a budget narrative is not required, use footnotes in your budget spreadsheet to identify sources and values of other funding.

Sample Budget and Narrative

Note that in this sample budget for a mobile media-laboratory project, it has columns for total cost, money requested from the funder, the nonprofit's contribution, and a "community match."

Community match, in this case, is listed separately. It indicates that ABC nonprofit understands that, in order to completely implement the project, it must identify and apply for additional funding contributions above those requested of this funder and provided by the applicant.

Also note that although purchase of a van and equipment is the first logical step in the process of launching a mobile media laboratory, the funder has already indicated that it does not issue grants to support capital purchases. Therefore, the organization applied for funding based on the stated interests of the grantor and is determined to seek capital funding elsewhere.

A budget narrative is shown following the grid sample and describes the rationale for each line item.

Line Item	Total Cost (two years)	Requested of City Foundation	ABC Match	Community Match
Capital Purchases				
Van and conversion equipment to include phone-switching equipment, storage, security, and generator	$30,000		$30,000	
Laptop computers and DVD players, server, printer, and scanner	$20,000	$5,000	$5,000	$10,000
Promotion				
Van printing and signage, posters, press kits, rental promotion, television and radio shots, collaborative planning, and promotion with community partners	$20,000	$10,000	$10,000	
Staff				
Vista/Americorps and Community Volunteers (equivalent)	$40,000	$40,000		

Line Item	Total Cost (two years)	Requested of City Foundation	ABC Match	Community Match
One FTE supervisory/ teaching staff to develop curriculum, deploy and operate program, and train staff and volunteers	$60,000	$60,000		
Maintenance				
Fuel, upgrades, Internet service fees, etc.	$10,000	$5,000	$5,000	
Overhead				
Staff and volunteer supervision, financial tracking and reporting, program oversight, and evaluation	$15,000	$5,000		$10,000
Totals	$195,000	$80,000	$50,000	$65,000

ABC Nonprofit provides $50,000 in-kind and cash match and requests a grant of $80,000 to launch the project described; $65,000 to fully implement the project and achieve the stated outcomes will be sought from ABC's community partners and foundations. Line-item detail follows:

Capital Purchases: ABC requires a van and equipment to launch the mobile media laboratory. A small portion ($5,000) of the total $50,000 capital expenditures is requested of the XYZ Foundation.

Promotion: The Mobile Media Laboratory is an opportunity for both ABC Nonprofit and the XYZ Foundation to build and enhance community relations. ABC, therefore, requests $10,000 from the XYZ Foundation for publicity, promotion, and community awareness. Furthermore, ABC will ensure that the project is called the "XYZ Foundation-sponsored Mobile Media Lab," a tagline that will be printed in all promotional materials and painted on the media van.

Staff: ABC has been granted the services of two Americorps volunteers whom it will assign to the project. The equivalent pay of an estimated $40,000 over two years is contributed by ABC to the project. ABC requests $60,000 from the funder to pay for two years' service from a project coordinator.

Maintenance: Ongoing maintenance and costs are charged to ABC and its community partners.

Overhead: ABC requests $5,000 of the $80,000 grant award to be allocated for fiscal oversight and program reporting.

Community Match: ABC Nonprofit and its technology planning partners described in this proposal are in the process of applying to area foundations and corporations for support of a comprehensive project to narrow the digital divide.

As a part of that overall plan, the mobile media-lab project will receive portions of support granted to the partners. Other funding sources will include rental revenues and reduced costs for staffing afforded by the use of community and recently granted Americorps/Vista volunteers.

Chapter 15

Other Grant-Proposal Sections

Every RFP or set of guidelines has, by one title or another, a section on the community or market need, a project description, an evaluation, and a budget. Beyond that, however, you may be asked to respond to numerous and varied questions.

What You May Encounter and Where

Although government grants, particularly federal ones, tend to want more detail in your narrative than foundations, you will find a wider variety of subjects to address among established foundations.

This is due, in part, to the establishment of a standardized common grant-proposal format by many Regional Associations of Grantmakers (RAG) and their member foundations. Because each foundation had input in the creation of the standard, the hybrid is far more comprehensive in its scope of questions than any one of the individual foundation's guidelines was before the standardization.

Many subject areas (educational programs, medical programs, technology transfer) have special questions asked in no other requests for proposals. For instance, educational-grant providers often require a section on professional development to ensure that teachers are prepared to deliver the program described.

Medical-grant RFPs may require a section responding to issues uncovered in an annual site visit and particular only to your clinic. You might be asked to address sanitation measures implemented or the availability of foreign-language interpreters during medical visits.

Technology transfers, medical grants, and experimentation grants always require sections on testing in human or animal subjects.

Specialized sections that may appear on some more technical RFPs require specialized, and often expert, knowledge of the subject matter. Seek assistance in writing these sections.

We've selected those sections that are most common and more applicable to a number of different types of projects. You are likely to encounter one or all of these at some point in your quest for grants.

Collaboration/Partnership

Both government and foundation grantors hold collaboration and partnership in high esteem; they believe there's a cost savings in collaboration. While technically that still has to be proved, it is a cost savings to them because they are not funding two agencies to do similar projects or to address similar needs among identical populations.

Whenever possible, identify collaborative links in your community. Local funders know when you don't attempt to partner because they know pretty much everything that is going on in the community. State and national funders will know you aren't talking to others when they receive two RFP responses from the same geographic area. Politically, the worst thing your organization or employer can do is know that another agency in town is developing a project similar to yours and not extend a request for partnership.

When You Partner

In a section on collaborations and partners, if requested, provide a narrative that:

- Lists the partners to the project
- Provides a brief description of each partner's role in the project
- Justifies the existence of the collaborative—why it was formed and "the beauty of it"
- Names a lead agency and/or a fiscal agent: The fiscal agent is the only organization that will receive funds. It will then purchase or pay for services from the other members of the collaborative.

Insider Tip

If appropriate, chronicle the history of collaboration between the organizations

Stating that the collaborative was formed to respond to an RFP requirement, even if it's true, is not a good idea. A collaborative should come together primarily to address a community issue, and only secondarily to seek grant funds to support its problem-solving efforts.

What If There's No Partner?

No partners or collaborators? Here's a short sample response from one such agency. Note that it addresses the need to coordinate services even though it does not directly partner with others:

ABC collaborates with hundreds of area agencies to develop and/ or deploy the assistance necessary in order to improve the lives of individuals and families in the target areas. ABC's role is to work with neighbors and community-based organizations to identify priority concerns and necessary remedial services, and to secure those services from the existing system rather than to duplicate what already exists. ABC also provides community outreach and public awareness in the target areas for the services provided by other agencies.

Review of Literature

A review of the literature is exactly that—a review of the research on a topic, cited and stated to support your case and explain the reason you selected the model for service that you did.

Federal departments, such as the departments of education or health and human services, and some selected medical-project funders, are among those grantors that require a review of literature. Especially in highly specialized areas such as medicine or electronics, if you are not well versed in the field, it is best to work with a professional researcher and/or expert in the field. It is often critical in specialized areas that you cite all the literature available on a subject. For a layperson, that search can be as exhausting as it is exhaustive.

Following is an abbreviated sample provided by an expert resource to a grant writer.

Lead poisoning has become an increasingly significant public-health issue. According to the U.S. Centers for Disease Control and Prevention (CDC), nearly one million children in the United States have levels of lead in their blood high enough to cause irreversible health problems and to produce a variety of developmental challenges.

Research has shown that lead poisoning has a pervasive impact on the human body, impacting most of the physiological systems. Those most affected include the central nervous system, reproductive system, kidneys, and other (organs). At the higher levels, lead poisoning can cause coma, convulsions, and even death. But even at the lower levels, the presence of lead in the blood can severely limit a child's development. Some of the most significant consequences include diminished intelligence, limited neurobehavioral development, diminished physical growth and stature, and impaired hearing.

However, lead poisoning is completely preventable. Unlike many public-health challenges, the environmental hazards that contribute to lead exposure can be abated and the threat of lead poisoning reduced. The only requirements are a willingness to invest in at-risk neighborhoods and a commitment on the part of key stakeholders at a national, state, local, and community level.

During the past decade, a variety of efforts have been initiated in neighborhoods across the country to remediate lead hazards and track the impact of these remediation strategies on public-health indicators. In the City of Baltimore, for example, the city government has joined with nonprofit and development organizations to address lead hazards in the home.

The primary weakness of many of these efforts, though, is that they fail to make connections among key stakeholders. Most have very little direct involvement by residents of affected neighborhoods and/or lack the necessary investments on the part of national organizations. Also, many of the initiatives fail to involve stakeholders from the public-health or medical communities, or from research institutions, which prevents them from tracking the impact of their efforts or advancing knowledge of lead poisoning in the scholarly community.

A review of existing literature on lead hazards results in numerous publications on risk analysis, lead hazard control, primary prevention strategies, and global prevention strategies. Little literature exists on the development of broad-based collaborations to ameliorate exposure and risk or on the potential for effectiveness of such collaborative efforts.

Note that the introductory paragraph states the number of children affected from national data. The author draws on further medical research, detailing why lead poisoning is a cause for concern. And again, by drawing on national statistics and a review of literature on lead-abatement projects in other cities, the grant writer makes a case for how the proposed program will be different and why it is likely to be successful.

Reviews of literature for social or educational projects are much easier. Locate materials about the service model to use in your project description. Compare the selected service model with one or two others and tell why the one you selected is more appropriate to the needs of your population than the other. Cite your resources (if possible, four or five) and attach a bibliography to the narrative if requested.

Staff Qualifications

This is a relatively simple section to respond to. Use the resumes of those working on the project staff to summarize their relevant experience. If their resumes are outdated, interview them briefly about more recent accomplishments. If the staff position is not filled, write a job description; list the responsibilities the person in that position will have and the qualifications of a successful applicant for the position.

Try to be sure that the staff and the board of the nonprofit organization for a project reflect, in gender and ethnicity, the target population.

Insider Tip

If you are requesting grant funds for a position, you must outline the job responsibilities and discuss at length the type of person the agency will be seeking. Be sure to include a brief plan for a personnel search and an equal-opportunity statement from the bylaws of your organization when requesting funding for staff positions.

Management Plans

The narrative describing management plans should center on the project rather than the entire organization. Do include, however, an overview of the organization and demonstrate where the proposed project fits into its mission and management structure. Illustrate reporting channels with graphs or organizational charts. Describe who is accountable for what aspect of the programming, and be sure to include a statement about fiscal accountability as a part of the management plan.

Let's look at a sample management plan. The following plan to improve and restructure a high school outlines the roles and duties of various personnel and administrators who will enable the district to meet its goals and objectives.

The high school principal will provide leadership in the high school community by building and maintaining a vision, direction, and focus for student learning. He will foster an atmosphere that encourages teachers to take risks to meet the needs of students. The superintendent and other administrators, with school-board members, will exercise leadership in supporting the planning, implementation, and long-range momentum of improvement at the school level. Teachers will provide the leadership essential to the success of reform, collaborating with others in the educational community to redefine the role of the teacher and to identify sources of support for that redefined role.

Planning and implementation for the high school restructuring improvement is under the leadership of sixteen committees composed of community representatives, out-district educators, teachers, parents, students, and administrators.

Each larger grouping of committees (such as "school environment" or "assessment/accountability") has selected one of its committees to participate with a leader to consider requirements for accreditation.

Ultimately, district administrators and the high school principal will be responsible for ensuring the success of the restructuring and its outcomes for student learning. However, the team approach ensures that staff, students, and community are responsible for the success of this effort.

Competing Programs/Agencies

Here's the Catch-22 on discussing your competition: If you list competing programs and/or agencies, you will have to say why they are not partners to the project. If you don't list them, the funder—particularly if it's a local foundation—will likely surmise that you are creating the project in a vacuum and deny your request.

Of course, the best-case scenario is when you have no competition. But most often that's only true if all of the competitors are part of a collaborative addressing the same issue. That leaves you with only one way to "win" this one.

Acknowledge what others in the community are doing, then describe the ways in which your organization or this particular project is different from what others are doing and/or ways in which the similar organizations remain specialized but are coordinating their efforts.

You can say: "LMNO, RST, and XYZ offer services for youth in the inner city; however, ABC is the only organization in the city to work in conjunction with the city police department and to provide police officers as mentors and coaches for youth in all of its programs.

"ABC's Camp was the first of its kind in the state to provide summer camping for low-income youth. Today, staff know of several camps providing experiences for at-risk and/or low-income children and adolescents, including GEF, LMN, and ZYX. Like the inner-city youth centers, however, ABC's camp has always been unique in that police officers participate with youth at camp as day counselors and coaches." With that, you've set your program apart from the others.

Constituency Involvement

You may be asked to describe constituency involvement in the design of the program, in its evaluation, in its execution, or even in all three. Also, you may see this same request with different phrasing. For example, schools are asked to describe "parent involvement" and hospitals to describe "patient input."

Foundations are no more eager than nonprofit organizations to "impose" services on a population. Involving those individuals most affected by the program in its design, delivery, and evaluation is a good way to both capture a funder's attention and ensure the success of the effort.

Consider this section this way: How would you feel if someone gave you a secondhand pair of shoes without ever asking you if you needed or wanted them? How would you feel if your local phone company came out with a statistic that said it had 100 percent customer satisfaction and you've had nothing but trouble with them? Wouldn't you say, "Well, they didn't ask me!"

Agencies should always consult with those in need to put a face on the statistics, to show that the program is designed in consultation with, rather than for, its beneficiaries.

Common Cents

Write about the involvement of program beneficiaries in your project description whether you've been asked to or not. This is a critical and politically charged issue for most funders, so even when they don't ask, tell them that you involve constituents or stakeholders in your program design and evaluation.

Make certain your client talks to the people who will benefit from the services and finds out if they need the services or even want them. Then write about their participation in the section on constituency involvement.

Sustainability Plans

Foundations and governments love to fund new and innovative projects, and in the past were reluctant to fund ongoing operations of a nonprofit organization. Today, however, some foundations are changing their approach and providing operating support to the nonprofit organizations deemed most critical to the continued vitality of their communities.

The biggest struggle among leaders in the nonprofit sector is finding operational funding to keep the doors open and the lights on, just so they can continue to do the good work they've already started. Often, they have created additional programs just to provide a portion of grant monies for overhead (or "indirect") costs. But that puts them in an awkward situation because the more programs they invent—assuming the programs work—the more they have to maintain.

You can understand that it can get a little tricky when you sit down to talk about how you're going to sustain a project over the long term, after it becomes institutionalized and, as such, the responsibility of an already stretched "operating" budget.

Why You Need a Good Plan

This section, nonetheless, is the make-or-break point of consideration among foundation trustees and grant readers. You must plan how you will put together the funding to sustain the program after the grant money is spent. You'll have to decide whether it will be through fees for service, partner funding, future grants or donations, operations, or, most likely, some combination of these income sources.

And often, you'll need a plan for sustaining the project for at least three years after the grant period ends.

The hard truth is that most projects really struggle when launch funding runs out. Often, they become a shadow of what they once were. The plus side of the equation is that the leadership of the organization can review its evaluation and eliminate what doesn't work. The negative side is that whether a program works just the way it is, any adjustment could weaken it and the agency that operates it.

All that said, you are left with the responsibility of writing something as realistic as possible under rather unrealistic expectations.

Sample Sustainability Plan

As you'll see in the following sample budget for sustainability, the agency tries to balance declining grant funds with increased fees for services. It also plans to seek local foundation funding to replace declining government funding and contribute some support from its own annual budget.

Year One: $432,500 Budget

grant year includes one-time capital investment

45-percent local funding	ABC annual budget	$75,000
	Fees for service	$3,000
	Existing grant	$80,000
	Donations and discounts	$40,000

*55-percent federal
grant-funding requested*

Year Two: $175,000 Operating Budget

100-percent local funding	ABC annual budget	$25,000
	Local grants	$100,000
	Fees for occasional services	$5,000
	Fees for regular service	$25,000
	Local underwriters	$20,000

Year Three: $175,000 Operating Budget

100-percent local funding	ABC annual budget	$30,000
	Local grants	$75,000
	Fees for occasional services	$10,000
	Fees for regular service	$35,000
	Local underwriters	$25,000

Year Four: $175,000 Operating Budget

100-percent local funding	ABC annual budget	$50,000
	Local grants	$30,000
	Fees for occasional services	$15,000
	Fees for regular service	$50,000
	Local underwriters	$30,000

This nonprofit was smart. The minute they were awarded a federal grant, they began meeting with local funders to talk about what they'd need in years two and three. Over the next year, they sent program officers media articles about the project and evaluation results, so they were well positioned to seek funding when the time came.

Status of Fundraising Efforts

This section is often requested in local grants. It is appropriate when you are raising a large total sum from several different sources. For instance, you'll be requesting $100,000 from the community foundation, $200,000 from area corporations and corporate foundations, and $50,000 each from a couple of key donors.

The grantor wants to know whether you have submitted proposals to those identified funders—remember, they know who they are and they talk among each other—and the status of those proposals (that is, proposals that are submitted, planned, pending, or funded).

A sample response for a capital project might read like this:

> The state provided $37.1 million toward the center's development; private donors have provided $16 million. The capital campaign became public with $4 million needed. The XYZ Corporation Foundation has since committed $500,000.
>
> Grant requests are pending with JJJ Family Foundation ($100,000 requested), NNN Foundation ($50,000 requested), and local philanthropist ($500,000 requested). Remaining corporate naming opportunities and a public "buy a brick" campaign are expected to raise the remainder of necessary funding.

Organizational History

Write this once, and you'll rarely have to write it again! No matter who the funder or what its priorities, the history of your organization is not going to change much and neither is the "slant" you put on the story. Be sure to put in highlights of the organization, as you'll note in the following example.

The City County Art Association was founded in 1910 by a City Federation of Women's Clubs, which recommended the establishment of an art collection as a basis for a future art museum. In 1911, an initial collection was assembled, and in 1924, the association occupied a Greek Revival residence, which was eventually renamed the City Art Museum (CAM). In 1981, the museum moved to its present site, a Beaux Arts–style Federal Building listed on the National Register of Historic Places and located in the city's downtown center.

CAM's core collection now consists of more than 6,000 works of art from all cultures and periods, with special strengths in European art from Renaissance to nineteenth century, nineteenth- and twentieth-century regional and American art, and works on paper including prints, drawings, watercolors, and photographs. The museum has always placed the highest importance on its public-education programs and continues to expand and diversify its classes, lectures, and events through collaborations and creative partnerships with other city institutions. The city's public sculpture program is supported by the museum's collection, which includes maquettes, drawings, and prints by major sculptors.

Use the history of the organization as a place to record changes in mission, growth of services, and other interesting and relevant facts. In some ways, the history can be used to justify the project, especially when you can cite continued growth or demand.

Funding Priorities

This section is the funder's way of asking, "If we can't fund you at the level you want us to, how would you like us to help you with a lesser amount?" There are several ways to handle this, as shown in the following examples.

When Less Won't Do

In this sample, the organization is steadfast in its request for funding at the level requested and offers only an alternative in the length of the grant period. Note that the writer emphasizes that a level of funding is necessary to meet the outcomes of the project and that any less would mean that those outcomes would not be accomplished as promised in the proposal:

> The project proposed would require an XYZ Foundation grant of $600,000—$143,000 to complete the year-one outcome objectives; $253,000 to achieve the year-two outcome objectives; and $204,000 in the final year—to complete the project as described. An alternative would be to structure a five-year plan which would allow smaller per-year investments toward a slightly slower developmental process.

When Any Amount Will Help

In the following sample response, the writer is saying, in effect, that whatever funding is available will be welcome and that the agency would appreciate the assistance of this funder in helping it get funding from other community sources.

> Whether or not funding is available at the level requested, the coalition hopes that the foundation staff will consider assisting us in building a partnership of funders to share the three-year financial commitment necessary to achieve the stated objectives.

Offering Choices

> This final sample offers the grantor some choices.

> If the XYZ Foundation is unable to grant the full three-year request, ABC Nonprofit offers two alternatives: the first two years' funding at $60,400 and $42,280 respectively for a total

grant of $102,680, or the executive-director salary only, in decreasing amounts as follows: $45,000 in year one, $31,500 in year two, and $22,050 in year three for a total grant of $98,550.

Challenge Grants

This is more likely a question than a whole section in the grant proposal. The funder wants to know whether you are applying for a challenge grant, meaning that you want them to put up funds that you can use to challenge or enthuse other potential donors.

For example, if you want to raise $50,000, you could ask for a $25,000 one-to-one matching challenge. A word of caution, however: Under challenge-grant agreements, if you don't raise $25,000 from other places, you don't get the $25,000 put up by the challenge funder.

Common Cents

A challenge grant provides money only in the event that you raise a like amount (or sometimes double amount) from others. Some foundations only offer challenge grants, some ask you if you would like one. In the latter case, don't ask for a challenge grant unless you are fairly certain you can raise the necessary match.

Say yes to a challenge-grant opportunity when you are:

- Launching a capital or fundraising campaign and want to use the challenge grant to attract attention among funders
- Entering the latter stages of a long fundraising campaign and want to challenge community donors to match one last gift
- Confident of your ability to raise the matching funds

If none of these is true, turn to former First Lady Nancy Reagan for inspiration and, "Just say 'no.'"

Chapter 16

Capital-Grant Proposals

Most nonprofit organizations undertake a capital campaign at some time during their growth to fund the construction or renovation of a building or the acquisition of costly equipment. These efforts—which often require millions of dollars and several years to realize—especially need the assistance of a savvy grant writer to supplement the work of staff development directors, the capital campaign cabinet, and consultants hired to guide the effort.

What Is a Capital Project?

Capital projects are those in which the primary goal is to purchase, build, or renovate a building, or to acquire high-cost equipment. Often, capital-project revenue goals are in the millions of dollars. In these cases, the nonprofit organization launches a "capital campaign" that requests money of constituents, businesses, foundations, and other community members.

Common Cents

The campaign cabinet may include some board members of the nonprofit, but it should also include community members who are used to asking others for money and who are known to donate to various causes. In fundraising, unlike in grantseeking, "who asks" is always the most important factor in your success or failure.

A capital campaign begins with a feasibility study, usually performed by an outside campaign-consulting firm. The firm asks potential donors what they think of the nonprofit's chances of raising the goal amount of money and then makes recommendations to the nonprofit about how to manage the campaign. The consulting firm and the nonprofit often next convene a team of community members who form the campaign cabinet and make calls on potential donors. Meanwhile, a grant writer begins developing proposals to submit to local foundations. Often, grant awards form the earliest donations to a campaign, signaling to other donors in the community that the project has potential for success.

Some campaign-consulting firms offer grant-writing services as a part of their campaign consulting; others leave it to staff or grant-writing consultants but advise them throughout the process.

Who Gives to Capital Campaigns?

Unless the nonprofit organization is a national one, almost all the money raised for a capital project comes from local funders, including foundations, businesses, and individuals. Capital projects sometimes get funding from the state if the project is a large public-use facility such as an arena, hospital, or convention center. State and federal governments do not generally provide capital in response to a grant application; capital allocations are often made as agreements between representatives and civic leaders. A grant writer can assist a capital campaign in securing government dollars by adding equipment purchases into relevant programmatic proposals.

For instance, a school might seek computers for staff under the federal Safe Schools–Healthy Students grant program as a part of a goal to increase communication among teaching staff and implement standards-based outcome reporting. The purchase of those computers might then reduce the needed budget of a capital campaign to build and equip a new middle school.

The Kresge Foundation in Southeastern Michigan is currently the only foundation that provides capital-grant funds to organizations without regard for where they are located. For several years, the foundation has structured its grants around a "capital challenge" requiring its applicants to identify new sources of funding in their local communities to match the Kresge grant and close out the campaign.

The Grant Writer's Role

Though every community and every project varies in who gives what and in what amount, often, the grant writer will raise up to half of the campaign goal through formal proposals to local foundations. The grant writer may also be involved in writing a case statement for the campaign brochure and in crafting letters the organization will send to various individual donors.

Insider Tip

Most grant writers, unless they are the directors of the nonprofit organization, don't get involved in organizing the campaign, performing the feasibility study, convening a campaign cabinet, or determining naming opportunities. Instead, these functions are left to the expert consulting firms to perform.

Naming Opportunities

Most capital campaigns include opportunities for donors to name the entire building, rooms within it, or other purchases made with donated funds. Some foundations like naming opportunities; others don't. Be sure to ask in your initial meeting with the foundation whether they wish their donation to be commemorated in a naming opportunity or in a more simple way such as a plaque in the building lobby.

Writing a Capital-Grant Proposal

Foundations do not give capital grants to purchase equipment or a building. They give grants to enable the nonprofit organization to do something important with the equipment or building. Remember that important distinction every time you write a capital-grant proposal. The most important thing to the audience is what the nonprofit will be able to do with what it purchases. Perhaps it will increase its capacity for providing service, enable staff to communicate and collaborate better with other organizations, or provide a new and necessary service. As with project grants, the outcomes from a capital-grant proposal must improve some currently undesirable condition.

Some foundations provide different guidelines for capital requests, and many ask for additional sections to be completed. For the most part, however, capital requests follow existing foundation guidelines, but the responses are somewhat different. Following are suggestions for how to approach the basic sections of a proposal when requesting funds for capital projects.

Problem or Need Section

You can copy the general case statement for a capital campaign into the need section of a grant proposal; they are that similar. Describe the need for the capital acquisition and use data to support your argument. A sample follows:

> The Great River City Media Center (CMC), located on the west side of Great River, State, is the premiere public-access media organization in the United States.
>
> Demand for CMC's services has increased as technology has changed. First, it added radio, then Internet and computer services, the I-VAN program for use in K–12 schools to teach digital filmmaking and editing, and a second television station, LiveWire 24, which broadcasts throughout the county with educational programming such as Classic Arts Showcase, NASA Direct, and Free Speech TV.
>
> As programs and demand have increased, so has CMC's staff—from twelve in 1997 when it moved from the Reed Library basement into the second floor of the west-side library on Bridge, to thirty in the early 2000s, when it had staff dispersed to a rectory and church basement next door to the library and to Steepletown, a west-side nonprofit-organization complex. From 1998 to 2002, community members' use of CMC grew as follows:

- GRTV (Great River TV) saw a 15-percent increase in locally produced programming. It grew from one broadcast channel to two and from one primary program to three with the addition of I-VAN educational services and Community Media Services video production and AV services.
- GRRadio grew from sixty-five to eighty volunteers; from five or six annual concerts to twenty-five to thirty.
- GreatNet grew from forty nonprofit "clients" to nearly 100.

CMC's programs and expansion would not be possible or necessary without the interest and commitment of community volunteers and public-access users. Before individuals or organizations get involved with public-access media, they attend an orientation about the CMC's radio, television, Internet, and media-literacy programs to determine their areas of interest. Though CMC has not promoted "orientations" in any formal way, demand for the introduction to the CMC's programs has grown in the past several years. Whereas, five years ago, an average of nineteen people attended the monthly orientation, now attendance averages thirty per session. This brings in more than 300 individuals annually to the organization. The community looks to CMC to take on the latest technologies and is therefore increasingly drawing individuals interested in podcasting, digital imaging, and Internet media.

Because the demand for I-VAN training in the schools has increased, CMC has done two things. First, it has established an I-VAN Club in the recently acquired storefront on Walter Street (formerly called the "annex") for the use of core-city young people. Second, it has developed teacher-training materials on DVD and CD that teachers can use to teach video production and editing in their classrooms. I-VAN staff are available by telephone and online to support teacher training and answer questions. In large part because of the success of I-VAN, CMC has identified a new niche that involves training K–12 teachers throughout the county to use media as a teaching and learning tool through the intermediate school district.

By 2002, CMC had outgrown its facility on Bridge Street. Staff were dispersed to three different sites, exchanging rent for CMC services. CMC began to explore possibilities for expanding in a way that would not disrupt services, but would, in fact, enhance them, and that would preserve the investment in technological infrastructure at the main office.

In 2004, the CMC was approached by key area funders and a neighborhood business alliance and asked to acquire and manage the historic Walter Theatre on the city's southeast side. The Theatre had been restored by a neighborhood organization approximately five years earlier. The restoration effort fulfilled the neighborhood organization's primary goal to serve as a catalyst for further revitalizing the Walter Street neighborhood. However, the Theatre had failed under several directors to sustain operations from programs, and its board of directors had looked for a resolution for more than six months before determining that it would surrender the property and a nearby facility they called the "annex" to an established nonprofit organization. The City Media Center appeared alone at the top of the list.

The acquisition of Walter Theatre and the annex was an opportunity to expand CMC's reach and visibility on both sides of the Great River and to fulfill several of the CMC's short- and long-range goals in that it offered:

- A venue for its concerts, televised debates, and other programs
- Additional space that was desperately needed following program expansion that had placed staff in three different sites on the city's west side

- Storefront access to CMC's educational programs and a presence in one of the city's most economically depressed neighborhoods

Evaluation

Evaluate the programmatic functions of the capital project. If a new building will increase the number of people your nonprofit is able to serve, design a means for gathering data and demonstrating that you have increased capacity for service within a specified time.

There are some capital efforts that do not involve programs. They are often public-works projects such as new sidewalks or public art or some other urban-renewal effort. It's difficult to establish evaluation criteria or tests of such capital projects. If the project has been built, clearly that is success. If it hasn't, the grantee should return any grant funds previously pledged. Nonetheless, foundations want an evaluation section in their grant proposals. In these cases, keep it simple—say that the project will be judged successful if it is constructed on time and within budget. Do not promise an evaluation just for the sake of evaluating. If you promise an evaluation, even one that doesn't make sense, the funder may hold you to your promise.

Unique Proposal Sections

Depending on the donor's requirements, capital proposals may include questions that you will not find in a foundation's typical guidelines. Common sections are relatively easy to complete or attach and include:

- A list of cabinet members
- A list of donors and their amounts
- A list of targeted requests by name and requested amount
- Architectural drawings
- Purchase agreements
- Proof of regulatory compliance
- Narrative description of existing and planned facilities

Common Cents

When a nonprofit organization undertakes a capital campaign, all members of the board, the campaign cabinet, and staff are expected to make a donation. Foundation donors want to see that those closest to the nonprofit have faith in the campaign and are investing their own money, too.

Writing a Program Plan

The most important component to a capital-campaign grant proposal is the plan both for how you will raise the necessary funds and how you will use new equipment or facilities. Following is a sample plan:

> The CMC's goal for growth, improvement, and acquisition of a venue was a perfect match with the request by the Walter Street Business District and other community agencies to explore and ultimately acquire the Walter Theatre properties. The capital campaign allows the acquisition and equipping of the Theatre, relocation of current staff who were dispersed in rented facilities, improvements and sorely needed updates to GRTV and GRRadio broadcast equipment, and high-tech network and broadcast connections between the two sites.
>
> The Theatre acquisition formed Phase I of the capital campaign. In Phase II, CMC seeks to "electrify" the Educational Center and Theatre to allow for remote broadcast of television and radio, install a media-making environment, and equip the Theatre with cameras and a control room. The Theatre will continue to be used for film, live performances, video, lectures, fundraisers, and other community-use purposes, and performances can be broadcast in numerous ways.
>
> CMC also plans to install a "hot studio" in a storefront in the Educational Center. It plans to link to the city's new wireless-Internet canopy to allow local residents and Theatre users Internet connectivity for asset mapping, community communi-

cation and development, job-search assistance, economic development, distance learning, and creative-arts applications.

CMC has developed a drop-in computer center for local residents, based on an expressed need from neighbors. The Center houses desktop computers and CMC's twenty-station mobile computer lab that is part of I-VAN. In the Educational Center, students can stop in after school and casually explore computer resources such as media production, educational games, research, and homework applications. I-VAN staff operate the drop-in center and the I-VAN Club for neighborhood youth who use digital-editing equipment to create video projects about curriculum subjects and neighborhood people, events, and businesses.

Once the Theatre and Educational Center are fully equipped and operational, CMC plans capital-campaign Phase III to include improvements and sorely needed updates to GRTV, LiveWire24, and GRRadio broadcast equipment, including digital conversion and digital network and broadcast connections between the CMC's Bridge and Walter Street locations.

Phase IV of the campaign includes construction of a two-truck garage and a maintenance endowment to be held at Great River Community Foundation.

The phases are prioritized by organizational and community need. As individuals and foundations have donated, CMC has completed portions of the project in accordance with donor wishes.

Chapter 17

Reviewing Your Work

The little details matter in a grant proposal. You've got the major items taken care of by now—the specifics of the program, the budget, the evaluation criteria—but you're not done yet. It is especially important to go over the proposal, focusing on the aspects that really give it that professional touch. This can make the difference between getting a grant and not getting a grant.

Spelling, Grammar, and Punctuation

No matter how good your spelling and grammar skills, you will need good reference books: a dictionary, thesaurus, and a stylebook or two (though no grant requires the use of one particular style over another). The Council on Foundations in Washington, D.C., has a stylebook particular to the philanthropy field, but it is geared more toward those writing about philanthropy than to those writing to philanthropists.

If your readers are going to judge just the content of the grant, which is their most appropriate role, you must proofread for errors before submitting your first draft. Check tenses, check punctuation and run-on sentences, and check your spelling. Use, but do not rely on spell check.

If you have enough time, walk away from your document for a day or two. Then proofread it again—that's when mistakes will jump out at you. If you are rushed, ask someone you trust to proofread the document.

Page Counts Count

Instructions in the RFP or grant guidelines almost always provide page limits, a list of what must be included within the page limits, or what is exempt from the limits. Follow all the formatting instructions carefully.

Insider Tip

Be sure to number your pages consecutively and to put the name of the organization and the city and state in all headers or footers. If a page gets misplaced, the proposal readers can either find it and put it in place or notify you or the granting agency that they cannot adequately score an incomplete grant application.

Using Headings

Once again, follow the directions. Use the same headings, and be sure to include the numbers, alpha characters, and/or Roman numerals used in the RFP. Do not, however, rewrite the instructions themselves or add the point value for each section.

Make the narrative as clear as you possibly can. Make your headings stand out by using bold, bold italics, underscoring, and other computer-enabled characters to separate sections, subheadings, and points. Do not use color.

Use bullet points for lists of items. However, here's a word of caution about bulleting. If the RFP instructions say to double space the proposal, everything—including the bulleted items—must be double spaced.

Evaluation Criteria

Judges use the evaluation criteria as guidelines when they award points to a project. These guidelines can be presented either as a list of criteria or as a rubric.

A rubric provides a scale for determining point awards to each section, according to how well it fits the description for that score. Following is a rubric for the abstract of an education proposal. The abstract in this case is worth up to 10 points.

Not Recommended	The project abstract is not included or is very incomplete.
Recommended for Funding with Revisions (3–5 points)	The project abstract minimally describes the project; portions of the required elements are missing or are labeled "see attached."
Recommended for Funding (6–8 points)	The project abstract contains all elements required (content/structure of project; number of students potentially benefiting; student identification process; assessment and evaluation). If ISD applicant, application indicates which local districts will participate in project.
Highly Recommended for Funding (9–10 points)	The project abstract contains all required elements and clearly and succinctly gives enough information so that the reader has an understanding of the scope, content, and structure of the proposed literacy achievement project and how it will be implemented and evaluated. If ISD applicant, application indicates which local districts will participate in project.

List of Criteria

Now let's look at a list of criteria. This list was established for a federal grant reviewer.

Criterion 1. Objectives and Need for Assistance (20 points)

1. The extent to which the applicant specifies the goals and objectives of the project and describes how implementation will fulfill the purposes of the Early Learning Opportunities Act (ELOA). The applicant must demonstrate a thorough understanding of the importance of early learning services and activities that help parents, caregivers, and child care providers incorporate early learning into the daily lives of young children, as well as programs that directly provide early learning to young children.

2. The extent to which the applicant demonstrates the need for assistance, including identification and discussion of its needs and resources assessment concerning early learning services. Relevant data from the assessment should be included. Participant and beneficiary information must also be included.

3. The extent to which the applicant describes its resources assessment and the relevancy of the results as the basis for determining its objectives and need for assistance.

4. The extent to which the applicant demonstrates how it will give preference to supporting activities/projects that maximize the use of resources through collaboration with other early learning programs, provide continuity of services for young children across the age spectrum, and help parents and other caregivers promote early learning with their young children. The applicant must provide information about how decisions will be made about who will provide each early learning service and/or activity funded through this grant.

5. The extent to which the applicant demonstrates that it has worked with local education agencies to identify cognitive, social, emotional, and motor-developmental abilities which are necessary to support children's readiness for school; that the programs, services, and activities assisted under this title will represent developmentally appropriate steps toward the acquisition of those abilities; and that the programs, services, and activities assisted provide benefits for children cared for in their own homes as well as children placed in the care of others.

Compare the Two

While a grant review is subjective, the evaluation criteria—however it is presented—is intended to make it less so. But the two different presentations of criteria somewhat encourage the reviewers to think differently.

Insider Tip

Grant proposals written according to guidelines, rather than to RFP, are generally not "scored." They are judged by how well they fit the guidelines of the foundation and fill a need or resolve a problem in the foundation's target area.

For instance, in the rubric form of evaluation, the section begins with no points and earns more as it goes up the scale. Compare that to the criteria list, where the need section began with 20 points and then lost points if it did not meet the expectations of the reviewer.

In some cases, the RFP will contain only a list of criteria for selection and no outline for the narrative. Follow the list of criteria exactly, using it as your outline. When you are provided both, use the evaluation criteria as a way of reviewing your work and as a tool for your readers to use to help you strengthen any weaker sections of the proposal.

Common Cents

In your schedule, be sure to build in enough time for review and revision of at least one draft of the proposal. Ideally, your team will read and judge two drafts before you submit the final. Give them at least three or four days with a draft—adequate time to review, digest, and provide feedback.

Competitive Priority Points

Many grant programs award competitive priority points for certain factors about the agency or its population. Usually, 5 points are available, over and above the score received on the proposal. They are awarded for such things as a high incidence of poverty among the population the organization serves, for being located in a designated economic-enterprise zone, or for some other criteria over which you have little or no control.

Even if you know you'll receive the priority points, do not add them to your evaluation scores. While the additional points can sometimes push you from "almost" to "funded," they don't strengthen your proposal or answer questions of grant judges.

Novice Applicants

Many federal grant programs are now awarding a competitive advantage to novice applicants. If your organization has never received a federal grant award, check the box on the cover sheet that indicates whether the organization is novice. While the proposal is not awarded additional points for being novice, it is given special consideration by the reviewers.

Chapter 18

Filling Out Forms

Writing the narrative may be the toughest part of completing the grant-proposal process, but the forms cannot be a last-minute task.

What to Expect

The number and types of forms accompanying a grant package vary, but you will always have at least two: a cover sheet and a budget form. Neither can be entirely completed until the grant package is nearly finished. Budget development takes place concurrently with the program development and is not final until late in the process. The cover sheet usually contains a budget-summary section, so that portion will not be ready early. You can and should, however, read the cover sheet much earlier so you can determine what information you will need to gather in order to complete the form in its entirety. Other forms that may accompany grant-application packages include the following:

- Assurances
- Checklists
- Project-summary form
- Certifications
- Informational grids

Federal grant RFPs usually have a separate packet of forms. If you download the RFP from the Internet, be sure to also download the "application," which will be provided as a separate document.

Grants.gov permits electronic applications. When you submit electronically, you must have prepared your cover sheets and other documents so you can complete the electronic forms completely. If they are not complete, the website will reject your submission.

Cover Sheets

Cover sheets request all or part of the following information:

- Name of organization
- Address of organization
- Name of contact person
- Telephone, fax, and e-mail address
- Brief summary of project
- Type of organization
- Signature of board chair
- Category of grant
- Federal tax ID and/or other special identity number
- DUNS number
- Signatures of CEO/executive director
- Scores of any surveys done to qualify for application
- Budget summary

Most of the information requested can be prepared in advance. You might want to fill out those portions of the form weeks before you have to submit the package.

XYZ Foundation
Street
Anywhere, USA

Grant Application (please type or print)
Organizations requesting XYZ Foundation funds must submit a
Treasury letter certifying 501(c)(3) tax-exempt status.
Date:
Organization: _____
Address:_____
Contact person's name:_____
Phone: _____
Contact person's title: _____

Purpose and objectives of your organization:

_____
_____
_____
_____

Normal funding/support sources:

_____

Geographic area served:_____
Client group served: _____

Title of project for which funds are sought and brief description of project, its objectives, goals, and benefits to clientele and
community.

_____
_____
_____
_____

Project dates: _____

Total project cost: _____

Amount and source of pledges/commitments to date:

_____

Other funding sources (and amounts) applied to for this project:

Amount requested from XYZ Foundation:

Has the XYZ Foundation supported your organization in the past?

If yes, specify dates and amounts:

If funds requested are for a new or pilot project, how are sustaining operations to be funded?

List XYZ corporate employees (or family) who are members of your board or volunteers in your organization:

List XYZ employees (or family) who are among your clientele:

Signed:

Date:

Identity Numbers

Cover sheets, particularly those supplied by federal and state grantors, request identity numbers. Foundations generally ask only for your 501(c)(3) letter and take the identifying number they need from that document. The identity numbers required by the government include, in some cases, the federal tax ID—as well as a special designation such as the number assigned a school district by the state—or the federal ID of a special-health clinic.

The federal government now requires a DUNS (Data Universal Numbering System) number on its cover sheets. This is a nine-digit number used to identify a business or nonprofit organization. The number provides access to financial information usually found in an organizational audit or other financial records and replaces the need to attach lengthy financial forms to your proposal. To look up your DUNS number go to *http://smallbusiness.dnb.com*.

Insider Tip

Be sure to look up or apply for a DUNS number early in the grant-writing process. While the system does respond quickly to an application or query, on rare occasions it can take up to two weeks to be assigned a number.

If your organization does not have a DUNS number, you can get one for free by calling 1-800-333-0505 or registering online at *www.dnb.com*.

Assurances and Certifications

Assurances are included in most federal application packets. They outline the enabling legislation and its parameters and describe the things that the applicant must already do in order to qualify for a grant. As grant writer, all you have to do is make a copy of the assurance and have it signed by the appropriate person (usually the executive director, chief executive officer, or similar position).

Certifications are similar to assurances, but they also may request additional information. For instance, schools are asked to certify that they are drug and violence free. The form requests a list of recent expulsions or disciplinary actions for drugs or violence on school grounds as well as the signature of the superintendent assuring the government that the school is addressing the problem.

Insider Tip

Sometimes you won't find instructions for writing a General Education Program Act (GEPA) narrative within the RFP. If you are writing a grant proposal from a school district, be sure to familiarize yourself with GEPA requirements and prepare this narrative in advance as a part of your writing assignment.

Schools must also provide a narrative response to GEPA requirements. The GEPA of 1994 requires all grant applicants to describe how they will provide "equitable access to, and participation in, its federally-assisted program for students, teachers, and other program beneficiaries with special needs." The statute highlights six types of barriers that can impede equitable access or participation: gender, race, national origin, color, disability, or age.

ASSURANCES AND CERTIFICATIONS STATE PROGRAMS:

Assurance Concerning Materials Developed with Funds Awarded under This Grant

The grantee assures that the following statement will be included on any publication or project materials developed with funds awarded under this program, including reports, films, brochures, and flyers: "These materials were developed under a grant awarded by the State Department of Education."

Certification Regarding Nondiscrimination under Federally and State Assisted Programs

The applicant hereby agrees that it will comply with all federal and state laws and regulations prohibiting discrimination and, in accordance therewith, no person, on the basis of race, color, religion, national origin or ancestry, age, sex, marital status, or handicap, shall be discriminated against, excluded from participation in, denied the benefits of, or otherwise be subjected to discrimination in any program or activity for which it is responsible or for which it receives financial assistance from the U.S. Department of Education or the State Department of Education.

Certification Regarding Title II of the Americans with Disabilities Act (ADA), P.L. 101-336, State and Local Government Services (for Title II applicants only):

The Americans with Disabilities Act (ADA) provides comprehensive civil-rights protections for individuals with disabilities.

Title II of the ADA covers programs, activities, and services of public entities. Title II requires that "No qualified individual with a disability shall, by reason of such disability, be excluded from participation in or be denied the benefits of the services, programs, or activities of a public entity, or be subjected to discrimination by such entity." In accordance with Title II ADA provisions, the applicant has conducted a review of its employment and program/service delivery processes and has developed solutions to correcting barriers identified in the review.

Certification Regarding Title III of the Americans with Disabilities Act (ADA), P.L. 101-336, Public Accommodations and Commercial Facilities (for Title III applicants only):

The Americans with Disabilities Act (ADA) provides comprehensive civil-rights protections for individuals with disabilities. Title III of the ADA covers public accommodations (private entities that affect commerce, such as museums, libraries, private schools, and day-care centers) and only addresses existing facilities and readily achievable barrier removal. In accordance with Title III provisions, the applicant has taken the necessary action to ensure that individuals with a disability are provided full and equal access to the goods, services, facilities, privileges, advantages, or accommodations offered by the applicant. In addition, a Title III entity, upon receiving a grant from the State Department of Education, is required to meet the higher standards (i.e., program accessibility standards) as set forth in the Title II of the ADA for the program or service for which it receives a grant.

In Addition:

This project/program will not supplant nor duplicate an existing early childhood development program.

Applicants not operating any component of the project directly must provide a letter of commitment and agreement, including the specifications of terms and conditions for delivery of services.

There is a written agreement between other eligible public nonprofit organizations or programs and the State that outlines provisions for the use of facilities for early childhood development program services (including such use during holidays and vacation periods; the restrictions, if any, on the use of such space; and the times when space will be available for the use of the applicant).

(Competitive Grants Only) The following provisions are understood by the recipients of the grants should it be awarded:

1. Grant award is approved and is not assignable to a third party without specific approval.
2. Funds shall be expended in conformity with the budget. Line-item changes and other deviations from the budget as attached to this grant agreement must have prior approval from a School Readiness Consultant of the State Department of Education.
3. The State Department of Education is not liable for any costs incurred by the grantee prior to the issuance of the grant award.
4. Grant recipients will comply with all subsequent legislation pending pertaining to this program.

Signature of Superintendent or authorized official:_____

Date:_____

Budget Forms

The federal government issues two types of budget forms: one for construction projects and one for nonconstruction projects. All social-service projects use the nonconstruction budget form, as the federal government does not issue RFPs for construction projects for that sector. The Department of Justice and some other more specialized departments have different forms, but the information requested is mostly consistent from one federal agency to another. Budget forms for federal grants are available when you download an application package at *www.grants.gov.*

Foundations often provide a budget form and a statement saying that if your budget is in a different form, they will accept it.

Most budget forms ask for the following line items:

- Personnel
- Fringe benefits
- Travel
- Equipment
- Supplies
- Contractual services/staff
- Training/professional development
- Indirect costs

Indirect costs are a set percentage (usually 5–10 percent of the grant budget) allowed in the grant for the proposing organization's overhead and grant administration. Read the directions to make sure that indirect costs are allowed before completing the budget forms.

Fitting into the Spaces Provided

Increasingly, foundations and government departments are providing interactive electronic forms, which can be filled out and changed at any time. However, some cover sheets are still available only as hard copies. Though these hard-copy documents can be completed by hand, they look far more professional if completed on a typewriter.

Admittedly, it isn't easy to line up all the little boxes and lines with the typewriter's keys and margin allotments—or even to find a typewriter these days. And, because you can vary type size and style only a bit on most typewriters, you'll find less space overall for keying in brief summaries, and even longer job titles, that must fit into the spaces provided. Do the best you can.

Insider Tip

You might want to make copies of the forms and complete them by hand first. Once you know what you want to write, type the responses on the originals. If you don't have a typewriter, check with your local library to see if they have a machine for public use.

With electronic forms that you get online, you have a bit more flexibility because you can change the size of the type or the font to fit into tight spaces. Forms sometimes allow a fixed amount of space for a brief narrative summary. And when you've entered about 200 or 250 words, you might discover the form simply won't let you write any further. Therefore, before you even get started, you'll want to develop a tightly worded, concise narrative summary.

Use the word or character-count function provided in most word-processing programs to make sure your text will fit into the space allotted on electronic forms or submissions.

Getting Signatures

As with support letters, you must begin planning for forms as soon as you receive the RFP. All of them request the signature of the chief person in charge of the organization, so you must coordinate schedules to get those signatures. Most forms also require the signatures of finance directors, program managers, and/or board presidents. Don't be surprised if you spend an entire day tracking down all of these individuals to get their signatures.

Insider Tip

Have officials sign their names in blue ink so you and the granting agency can tell quickly which is the original copy and which are the duplicates. Use this tip when asking officials to sign forms, support letters, audit reports, and other documents requiring original signatures.

You must always submit one original application and whatever number of copies are requested if you are submitting paper copies to the federal government. The original must contain original signatures from all the parties requested.

Chapter 19

Packaging and Submitting Your Proposal

Finally, you've completed the narrative and you're ready to complete the grant application package. Add the finishing touches, write the abstract, compile the last of the forms and attachments and ship or deliver it to the funder. Whew! You're almost done!

Writing an Abstract or Summary

Though an abstract or summary is one of the core components of all grant proposals, it's placed here because most grant writers find it easier to write the summary after the proposal is completed. Instructions for an abstract will be very succinct. The funder will want a brief description of the project, the need for the project, and the means of delivering the project (such as a collaboration or a qualifying statement about the applicant organization). In other words, they want a one- or two-sentence summary of each of the lengthy sections of your grant proposal.

The directions for the abstract will include a note regarding length either in number of words you are allowed or in terms of a page limit. You're rarely allowed more than one page, however, and often even less. Sometimes an abstract form is supplied by the granting agency. This will include a header with the name of the organization and its identifying number and sections for summarizing specific parts of your narrative.

Insider Tip

Write the abstract last. You've already done the work, and you just have to go into the narrative of the proposal and find some succinct sentences or paragraphs and paste them into the abstract. Then write just a few sentences to "glue" it all together.

Writing Cover Letters

Federal grants and state grants really don't require cover letters, but it's a nice gesture, even if you suspect they may be tossed in the trash by the person who opens the package. Cover letters are very appropriate for local foundations as this is your opportunity to make a personal link between the board or staff of the foundation and the board or staff of the nonprofit organization.

Start every letter with a "Thank you." It's a much nicer greeting than "I have enclosed," because it focuses on the reader rather than the sender.

Have the person in the organization with the closest link to the funder sign the letter. For instance, if a board member is a close personal friend of a trustee of a family foundation, ask that person to sign the cover letter. If there is no one with a personal link to the foundation, have the letter signed by the CEO or executive director.

Using Color, Photos, and Other Graphics

Graphic elements are always nice, as long as they can be included in the document and be contained within the page limits. Charts and graphs can be used to illustrate a process, to define the management structure of your organization, or to describe the workings of new inventions. In general, however, avoid the use of color graphics or photos, and try to avoid the need to illustrate your concept in color—use shading or line art instead. There are two reasons for this: First, if you must make copies in color, it is more expensive. Second, even though you've attached the requested number of copies, the funder often makes more copies, and they will not make color copies. In general, consider color prohibited unless you are instructed otherwise in the RFP.

Using Dividers, Binders, or Bindery

Once again, let the directions dictate your course. Most often, however, the grantmaker will prohibit bindery or special covers. Instead, they will direct you to staple the pages together or enclose them in a rubber band.

Stapling can create a problem when you have a lot of pages to fasten together. You can use a heavy-duty stapler that can staple through at least 150 pages. Rather than investing in equipment that you may use only infrequently, go to your local shipper or copy shop and use one the business provides for customers.

Sometimes the instructions ask you to three-hole punch your original and copies and to secure them with clips or rubber bands. That means that the granting agency intends to create binders for the reviewers. If you want to avoid having to hole-punch dozens or even hundreds of pages, you can buy a ream of prepunched paper for printing your proposal.

When a funder is not specific about binding or dividing copies, you are free to package your proposal as you wish. There are a number of different ways to do this:

- A three-ring binder with dividers for each section (This method is particularly effective when you have large grant proposals of more than 100 pages, such as those for medical or dental programs.)
- Wire or plastic bindery with a full-color cover or a simple cover with titles, logos, and other appropriate information
- A pocket folder with a cover letter in one pocket and the proposal and attachments in the other
- Binder clips

For the most part, keep your packaging simple. Often, even though you send the requisite number of copies, the granting organization must make additional ones. In these cases, they'll have to unbind or unstaple your grant packages.

Attachments and Appendices

Attachments and appendices are generally allowed (and sometimes required) and rarely count against your page limits. Sometimes the granting agency will limit the number of pages in your appendix and attachments. In this case, select the very best of your optional or limited attachments, such as support letters or media stories. Examples of attachments include:

- IRS determination letter—proof of 501(c)(3) status: required by foundations
- Board roster: required by most foundations
- Letters of support: required by most grantors, especially when you are proposing a collaborative structure
- News articles about the program: not required
- Annual report of organization: not required
- Organizational charts
- Maps
- Most-recent audit statement and report: often required by foundations; not required or wanted by federal government

Appendices might include such things as:

- Progress reports
- Formal needs-assessment reports
- Survey results
- Translated materials

Appendices are not required by most foundations. Only a few federal grant programs request appendices, and they will be clear about the content.

With the exception of the National Endowment for the Arts (NEA), few federal or state grant programs allow attachment of film or video. Most foundations don't appreciate video attachments unless they specifically request them. If you have an interesting, relevant video, place it on your website and reference its availability in your proposal.

Electronic Submissions

More and more, both the government and foundations are offering—and in some cases mandating—electronic proposal submission. Most still accept either a mailed document or the electronic submission, and some require both an electronic submission and mailed supplementary documents. Benefits of submitting your proposal electronically include:

- An extra day to complete the application
- No cost for mailing/shipping, unless for supplementary materials
- Most electronic-submission services will prompt you if parts of the application are missing
- E-mail confirmation of receipt of the document

Drawbacks may include the following:

- Unreliable connections to server
- Sometimes no means of saving the text, so must be completed in one sitting
- Registration can be complicated and time consuming

Electronic submission of documents requires that you create PDF files of your IRS designation letter, audit, and other required attachments. Usually, when you work in the electronic-submission format, you may go back and change the text as needed. Until you are finished, do not select the button that says "submit."

A couple more important points about using Grants.gov:

- Grants.gov requires a password consisting of upper- and lower-case letters, numerals, and symbols. Be sure to put your password in a safe place where you can look it up when needed.
- Grants.gov does not accept registration by individuals, so if you are an independent grant writer, the organization you are working for must register its own name, password, and contact information. You will not receive confirmation of submission, but your client will.

Making and Marking Copies

Government grants always tell you in the RFP how many copies to submit. They will also often tell you that the stated number is not required but "will facilitate review." This is really just a nice way of saying, "Send us the exact number of copies we requested." Foundations often do not say how many copies they'd like. Either call the program officer and ask, or submit one original packet.

Those agencies that require copies also require an original. Be sure that your original document is clearly marked as such. Use one or more of the following ways to indicate the original document:

- Add a sticky note with the word "original" to the original document.
- Print the original on stationery-quality paper and the copies on copy paper.
- Add colored sheets to the top of each proposal, with one color for the original and another for all copies.
- Attach a cover letter on organizational letterhead on the original document only. Do not attach a copy of the cover letter to any of the others unless it's requested.
- If binding, add a note to the cover of the package. Or make one color cover for the original and different color covers for the copies.

Shipping and Delivery Options

Other than electronic submission, there are three ways to deliver grants: personally, by mail, or by shipping service. The best choice among the three is the one that guarantees you'll meet the deadline.

For local grants and sometimes state grants (if you live in or near the capital city), the best option is hand delivery.

When the grant RFP states that a grant must be postmarked by a date, you must use the U.S. Postal Service. Dates entered into a shipping form do not count! When the RFP states that the grant must be received in the grantor's office by 5:00 P.M. on a certain date, you have to select the method that is most certain to get it there.

Since you will often be working on a grant, its forms, or its attachments on the very last day before it's due, you will probably use overnight shipping as a means of delivery to remote destinations. Use UPS or FedEx for these shipments. Unlike the postal service, these shippers provide a tracking number so you can know for certain when the grant has arrived. Please be aware, however, that if the shipper fails to meet the deadline, you can recoup the cost of shipping, but not the hours of labor and the potential for a large grant award. If at all possible, try to ship the grant two days before it's due.

The most critical thing about wrapping up the grant is ensuring that it arrives on time. Know the time of the last mail pickup or how late your overnight shipping service is open. Check to make sure the hours aren't going to change, and keep track of Sundays and holidays that can delay shipping.

Chapter 20

What Comes Next?

You've met the deadline and shipped the proposal. Big "Whew!" and congratulations! Take a brief breather, then prepare to tackle the next steps. If the grant is awarded to you, congrats! There's lots to do. But even if you don't receive the grant this time, there are steps you can take to ensure you have a better chance the next time.

Why Proposals Fail

There are several reasons that a proposal can be denied, including the most obvious and usual—that it did not score high enough to be in the top portion of projects submitted. Other reasons are not so obvious. For instance, proposals can be turned down because of any of the following:

- The client received a grant recently from the same funder, and the funder wishes to give others a better chance, even though it likes the project you are proposing.
- It's not your turn. Some grants, particularly state grants, appear to be distributed based on a rotating system of every three or four years.
- The organization did poorly on a past evaluation or failed to comply with the grant agreement on a past grant, even if the grant was from a different funder—don't forget, they often communicate with each other!
- The funder has a political agenda.
- The project did not fit the guidelines closely enough.
- Your community does not have the highest incidence of need.

- The funder's priorities shifted, or the program emphases changed.
- A similar project was just funded in your specific geographic area.
- You failed to follow the directions.

Requesting Reviewer Comments

Local foundations often will tell you what went wrong in the decision-making process during the trustee meeting. There is little you can do unless foundation staff give you some tips about reframing your proposal and invite you to resubmit the proposal.

In the case of state and federal grants especially, the first thing to do about a failed grant is to request reviewer comments if they were not shipped with the declination letter. Send a letter to the granting agency on your organization's letterhead. Include the number of the program, the date of the proposal deadline, and a polite request for reviewer comments and scoring.

Reviewer comments can range from a sheet of criteria with a square for a score and two lines per criteria for comments, to several full pages of narrative reviewer comments on each section of the proposal.

You'll find that if there were three reviewers, scores and comments will differ, sometimes drastically, among them. Where one reviewer might give you full points for a section and make no suggestions for improvement, another may cut your points by half and find fault with nearly everything you've done. Then they seem to switch views in the next section of the proposal. Your final total proposal scores from each reviewer, however, should fall within a few points of each other.

You may not contest low scores—even in the rare instance that only one of your reviewers has scored the proposal poorly. However, these comments are invaluable as a roadmap for strengthening your next attempt.

Rewrite and Resubmit the Proposal

You will have several months to absorb reviewers' comments and con-template how you will address their concerns in your next attempt. When you sit down to rewrite the proposal, ignore the strengths, or positive comments and address the weaknesses.

Some very technical grants, like the SBIR, require you, on a second application, to respond directly to reviewer comments and state how you've addressed the concerns they had with the project when it was first presented. However, most of the time, you will use the reviewer comments to improve your proposal in a much-less structured way.

Focus specifically on reviewer comments and address each throughout the revision—even if only one reviewer cited the topic as a weakness and another complimented it. If the evaluation section was weak, take it to the local university and speak with a professional evaluator. If the need section was weak, locate more data to support your case. If the project description requires more detail, work with project staff to strengthen the approach.

As a general rule of thumb, one revision and resubmission is man-datory with the permission of your client or employer. A second, if your revision is denied, is all right. If the second revision is also turned down, however, you may need to look at developing an entirely new project. Clearly, the weaknesses lie with what you are proposing, not how you are proposing it.

You Got the Grant—Now What?

There's a saying among leaders of nonprofits: "Darn, we didn't get the grant. Darn, we got the grant." Of course, everyone is happy to hear that they submitted a successful proposal. On the other hand, now the real work begins—implementing the project and fulfilling the work plan.

The first thing you, as grant writer, are most likely to need to do when your organization gets the grant is review and possibly revise the project budget. Often, six months have passed between submission and the confirmation of funding, and things have changed. The organization may have purchased some requested equipment or implemented some phase of the project with other money. And often, too, the granting agent requests a new budget for final approval.

Sometimes you'll get the grant, but it's for less than the amount you requested. The funders do this for a number of reasons. They may have decided to fund more projects than they originally anticipated and want all of you to reduce your overall budgets by 10 percent—you choose where. Or maybe they've declined a line item in your budget because they didn't want to fund that particular thing.

Writing a Media Announcement

Once you've gotten a grant, you'll want to do a bit of publicity in the local media. Local grants often require a media announcement as part of the grant-agreement contract. Just as with grant proposals, media announcements—also called press releases—are formulaic. Always begin with a headline such as "Media Release." Then provide contact information (the name, address, e-mail address, and phone number of the person in the organization who fields questions or can tell the media more about the project).

Also in the heading, you have to say whether the release is immediate or to be held until a certain date so the media know they may not release the information to the public prior to that stated time. Center a headline that announces the grant and the amount to be received. Then start the story with a dateline, just like those in the newspaper, that includes today's date and the city and state.

A two-page news release is more than sufficient. And it absolutely should always include at least one quote from project staff or leadership. If possible, use another quote from the granting agency. Describe the project in a way that makes it sound exciting. Signal the end with three number symbols centered after the last paragraph (# # #).

The Progress Report

Many grantmakers require that you submit periodic reports of your organization's progress with the program that has been funded. Unless you are also implementing the project, take your list of goals and objectives and interview your client about their progress toward each. Include the following topics in all progress reports:

- Progress toward stated goals and objectives
- Changes in the environment, funding, staffing levels, or other factors that limited progress and the ways in which they did
- Unanticipated successes and the reasons for them
- Anecdotal evidence of success (stories from participants)
- Long-term sustainability plans and steps taken in the interim to sustain the project
- Use of funds
- Any special terms or conditions of the grant agreement
- Lessons learned

The federal government has developed a standard reporting form for many of its grants. On them, you report progress toward the benchmarks, objectives, and/or outcomes you promised in your proposal. The reports require little narrative. Try to download a reporting form before you write a federal proposal so that you are sure you are framing your outcomes in a way that can be measured on the reporting form.

Glossary

501(c)(3):
IRS: designation for nonprofit organizations, including religious, educational, charitable, organizations set up to provide social services. See "nonprofit organization."

509(a):
IRS: designation defining public charities.

abstract (also called project summary):
Brief description of project, the need for it, and the means of delivering services.

annual report:
Report published by a foundation that describes how grant funds were expended during the fiscal year.

application:
Cover sheets and forms that must be completed as a part of the grant package.

assets:
Holdings of a foundation in the form of cash, stock, bonds, real estate, etc.

assurances:
Forms that must be signed and submitted to the federal government stating that the organization practices equal opportunity,

has an environmental policy, or agrees to some other requirement of the granting department.

bequest:
Money that is set aside and given to an individual or organization after a person's death.

budget forms:
Line-item list of items to be funded, including personnel, wages and fringe benefits, projected travel expenses, training, etc. Form usually provided by grantor.

budget narrative:
Details pertaining to the budget. Explanations and justifications of proposed expenditures, including calculations, other sources of funding, distribution of funding, estimated or actual costs.

building campaign:
Fund drive to raise money for construction or repair of buildings.

bylaws:
Rules that govern how an organization operates.

capital:
Funding sought to support construction or renovation of a building or its infrastructure, or for large equipment purchases.

capital campaign:
Drive to raise and collect money/funds that will finance an organization's building or renovation project.

case statement:
Statement of need.

certifications:
See "assurances."

challenge grant:
Money that is donated to a nonprofit if other donors contribute a predetermined or matching amount.

charity:
Nonprofit organization that operates for the purpose of helping/benefiting a certain segment of society.

checklist:
Often funder provided, this lists the components that must be included in the proposal. Sometimes the checklist is submitted and sometimes it isn't. Check instructions.

cold calling:
Going to a foundation and describing a need in the community and how your agency would like to address the issue.

collaboration/collaborative effort:
Joining of several nonprofit organizations to address a shared goal or develop a joint project.

community foundation:
Foundation established by one or two individuals who then enlist the aid of others in the community to contribute to the

corpus—fund base—either through direct donations, legacies, or annual donations.

community match:
Contributions provided by local donors to support items in a project not covered by primary grant.

competing agencies/programs:
Others in the community that may have similar programs but are not partnering in the proposed project.

constituency:
In the case of grants, most often the beneficiaries of a project or the target population.

corporate donor:
A corporation that makes grants of cash or goods to nonprofit organizations.

corporate foundation:
Company-sponsored, private foundation that contributes to the community by using a portion of its profits.

corporate-giving program:
A company gift of merchandise or money that came out of the annual budget for charitable giving, not from a separate endowment.

corporate grants:
Money or merchandise that is given to nonprofit agencies by a profit-making business.

corpus:
Money endowed to a foundation by a wealthy person, family, or corporation to provide funding for agencies that serve the community at large.

Council on Foundations (COF):
National organization that supports philanthropy throughout the United States and provides services and publications to member foundations.

decline/declination:
Foundation/government entity denies a request for funding a proposal.

direct costs:
Actual cost to operate a proposed project.

discretionary funding:
Money allocated to high-level staff or trustees of a foundation that they may grant on their own.

endowment:
In the case of foundations, the corpus. Additionally, foundations may "endow" a nonprofit by providing money to be held in trust. The nonprofit then uses earned income from the trust to pay for ongoing maintenance or operations.

evaluation component/plan:
Description of how you will assess the project and determine its success or failure.

excise tax:
Annual tax that must be paid to the IRS by private foundations.

family foundation:
Established by one or two donors/entrepreneurs to ensure that future generations continue to practice philanthropy.

federal government departments:
The following federal departments are most often those that make and administer grants for projects:

- DHHS: Department of Health and Human Services
- DOC: Department of Commerce
- DOD: Department of Defense
- DOJ: Department of Justice
- ED: Department of Education
- EPA: Environmental Protection Agency
- NIH: National Institute of Health
- OSHA: Office of Safety and Health Administration

federal grant application kits:
A set of forms that accompanies an RFP.

federal grants:
Money that U.S. departments grant/give to nonprofits either through direct grants or through another agency, using pass-through funds.

Federal Register:
Collection of all RFPs expected to be issued by the federal government in a given year. It is published or updated annually.

foundation grants:
A source of funding from private or public charitable trusts.

funding cycle:
The annual cycle by which foundations make grants (such as annually, tri-annually).

fundraising:
Overall effort by an organization to raise funding, including but not limited to grant seeking, special events, year-end requests for support, bequests, and building relationships with major donors.

gap analysis:
Used when there is not a lot of data to support need statement; looks at current situation, identifies desired outcome and what's missing, or the barriers to meeting goals.

goals:
Broad, overall purposes of a project.

government grants:
Tax dollars that the government (usually federal or state) redistributes to communities through programs.

grant:
A financial or valued gift made to enable a project.

grant proposal:
Documents written and used to apply for funding for a specific project or purpose.

grantee:
Organization that receives a grant.

grantor:
Organization that awards a grant.

grant-seeker workshop:
Workshops targeted to specific RFPs and sponsored by a funding agency to provide additional information about the proposal process.

grant seeking:
The process of reviewing possible funding sources and narrowing the field of likely prospects.

grant-writers workshop:
Workshop held by a granting agency, usually state or federal government, to receive peer/expert assistance in developing your writing skills.

grant writing:
The preparation of narrative, budget, and applications for funding.

guidelines:
Usually provided by foundations, the outline of types of projects or categories of projects the funder will and will not be interested in funding. Guidelines provide directions for submitting an application for funding.

identity numbers:
Tax identification or other identity number assigned to an organization by the federal or state government.

independent foundation:
Usually founded as a family foundation; a large foundation led by a board of trustees nominated from within but generally not composed of remaining family members of the donor.

indirect costs:
Costs that a nonprofit may take from project grants to pay a portion of overhead or operational expenses. Usually awarded as an allowable percentage of the project budget.

in-kind contribution:
Support offered by agency and partners to project, providing such things as staff time, office or other space, utilities, volunteer hours, and products.

IRS:
Internal Revenue Service.

IRS designation:
The letter indicating 501(c)(3) assignment status from the Internal Revenue Service. A copy of this document is most often required by foundations with the grant application.

LEA:
Local Education Agency (such as school district, intermediate school district, etc.).

letter of inquiry:
Describes a project and asks for permission to submit a grant proposal; the first step in the grant-proposal cycle.

letter of intent:
Tells the granting agency that you plan to respond to an RFP.

letter of support:
Written by a partner organization, community leaders, program collaborators, and recipient organizations in support of the proposed project for which you are seeking funding.

leverage:
Money or items required to qualify for a grant.

management plans:
Narrative supporting plans for managing a project.

matching-gifts program:
The means by which the match requirement will be met. See "matching grant."

matching grant:
A grant that's tied to the requirement that the applicant either use funds from its budget or raise donations of a certain amount in order to qualify for the grant.

multiyear requests:
Grants that are applied for once but awarded for several consecutive years of funding.

need statement:
Sets the stage for the proposal by describing your community, the target population, grant-seeking organization and what it does, and other relevant data that supports the need for the project.

NGO:
Nongovernmental organization or a nonprofit organization that is in no way affiliated with government, except in that it might receive funds from government.

nonprofit organization:
An organization designated by the Internal Revenue Service (IRS) as meeting the criteria (specifically, does not make a profit out of scale with its costs and performs a necessary function in society) for nonprofit status. Also referred to as a 501(c)(3), its IRS designation.

nonsupplanting funds:
Funds that may not take the place of operating costs. For instance, if the organization is paying for a staff position, it may not, if it is prohibited from supplanting, make the position a grant-funded one.

objectives:
Measurable means of achieving the goals of a project.

operating support:
Support for nonprofit operations (rent, utilities, staffing, etc.).

partnerships:
See "collaboration."

pass-through funds:
Funding that is available usually through a federal or state grant that is administered by a local government agency or local foundation.

payout requirement:
Amount (usually 5 percent of corpus) that foundations are required to pay out in grants annually.

philanthropy/philanthropist:
An organization/individual who donates money, goods, services, or time to humanitarian efforts.

post-grant evaluation:
Project evaluation made at the end of the grant period.

preliminary proposal:
Response to an RFP that calls for two papers: The first (preliminary) is used to judge which organizations may submit a full proposal for funding. Usually used for demonstration projects.

private foundation:
Also known as a private charitable foundation; it engages in giving to community agencies money that comes from a wealthy person, family, or corporation.

private independent foundation:
Often started by a family, but no longer controlled by donor or family members; administered by a board of trustees; the largest foundations in the United States; grants often made worldwide.

program officer:
Person who reviews grant requests at a foundation and makes recommendations for funding or not to the board of trustees.

project budgets:
Budgets for a specific project. Includes direct costs and indirect costs.

project manager:
The lead manager for a project.

RAG (Regional Association of Grantmakers):
Member organization serving foundations in a given region. Keeps catalogs and electronic databases of member foundations.

Request for Proposals (RFP):
A document outlining the types of projects the funder might be interested in funding, the criteria a potential applicant must meet in order to qualify for the grant, and the directions for submitting your proposal.

review criteria/evaluation criteria:
Guidelines or the rubric used by judges to judge the strength and value of a proposal and how that proposal will meet the grantor's objectives.

review of literature:
Review of research on a topic/issue; cited, and stated to support the case for a grant application and the reason that the model of service was selected; required by federal departments and some medical funders.

RFP:
See "Request for Proposals (RFP)."

rubric:
A chart that presents the evaluation criteria and assists the judges in scoring your grant.

seed money:
Initial funds that are used to start a project or fundraising campaign.

site visit:
Often a visit by foundation staff to meet the staff and see the operations of a potential grantee.

staff qualifications:
Summary of relevant service of staff who will administer proposed project.

state single point of contact:
Person or office in your state that catalogs who has applied for what grants and assists grant writers by responding to questions during the application process.

support letters:
Letters indicating contributions or support for grant applications.

sustainability plan:
Applicant's plan for raising money that will continue program after the original grant expires.

tax-exempt organizations:
See "501(c)(3)."

tipping:
When a nonprofit organization receives most of its support from one donor, it may "tip out" of its nonprofit status.

trustee:
A member of a foundation's board of decision makers.

Index